POINT OF NO RETURN
Tonkin Gulf
and the Vietnam War

POINT OF NO RETURN
Tonkin Gulf
and the Vietnam War

Earle Rice Jr.

620 South Elm Street, Suite 223
Greensboro, North Carolina   27406
http://www.morganreynolds.com

FIRST BATTLES

Lexington and Concord

Fort Sumter

USS *Maine*

Pearl Harbor

Tonkin Gulf

POINT OF NO RETURN:
TONKIN GULF AND THE VIETNAM WAR

Copyright © 2004 by Earle Rice Jr.

Library of Congress Cataloging-in-Publication Data

Rice, Earle.
  Point of no return : Tonkin Gulf and the Vietnam War / Earle Rice, Jr.

    v. cm. -- (First battles)
  Includes bibliographical references and index.
  Contents: Containing communism -- Defeat of the French -- Johnson takes
  charge -- Covert maritime operations -- Planning ahead.
    ISBN 1-931798-16-8 (library binding)
    1. Tonkin Gulf Incidents, 1964--Juvenile literature. 2. Vietnamese
  Conflict, 1961-1975--United States--Juvenile literature. [1. Tonkin Gulf
  Incidents, 1964. 2. Vietnamese Conflict, 1961-1975.] I. Title. II.
  Series.
    DS557.8.T6R53 2003
    959.704'31--dc21
                                    2003010709

Printed in the United States of America
First Edition

Contents

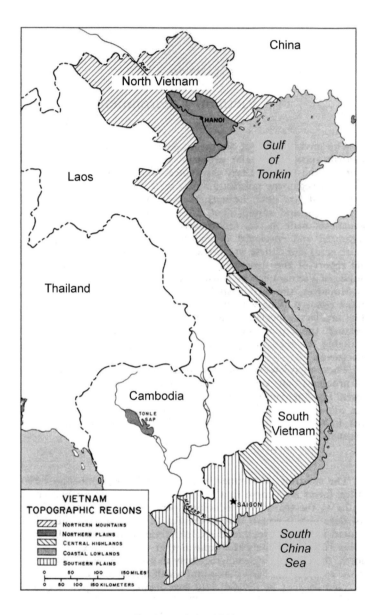

China

North Vietnam

HANOI

Gulf
of
Tonkin

Laos

Thailand

Cambodia

TONLE
SAP

South
Vietnam

VIETNAM
TOPOGRAPHIC REGIONS

NORTHERN MOUNTAINS
NORTHERN PLAINS
CENTRAL HIGHLANDS
COASTAL LOWLANDS
SOUTHERN PLAINS

0   50   100   150 MILES
0   50   100   150 KILOMETERS

SAIGON

South
China
Sea

Southeast Asia, 1964

Chapter One

Containing Communism

On August 4, 1964, at 11:36 P.M. eastern daylight savings time, a special news bulletin interrupted regular television programming. All three major networks announced President Lyndon Baines Johnson was about to address the nation on a matter of grave importance.

Shortly thereafter, the familiar image of the U.S. president appeared on screen. Staring solemnly into the television camera, he began reading a prepared speech from a teleprompter set up off camera. With his distinctive southwest Texas drawl he reported to his "fellow Americans:"

> As President and Commander in Chief, it is my duty to the American people to report that renewed hostile actions against United States' ships on the high seas in the Gulf of Tonkin have today required me to order the military forces of the United States to take action in reply.

The president went on to describe two attacks—the first taking place two days earlier on the U.S. destroyer *Maddox*, and a second reported attack occurring that very day on the U.S. destroyer *C. Turner Joy*. In response to the attacks, air action was "now in execution against gunboats and certain supporting facilities in North Vietnam which have been used in these hostile operations," he said.

While berating North Vietnam's "new act of aggression," the president informed the American public the time had come to let their enemies know "that our Government is united in its determination to take all necessary measures in support of freedom and in defense of peace in southeast Asia." To this end, he announced he would request the U.S. Senate and House of Representatives pass a joint congressional resolution supporting his efforts to halt Communist aggression in Vietnam.

Continuing, President Johnson acknowledged the encouragement of leaders of both parties and voiced his expectation for a quick passage of the resolution. He then thanked his Republican rival in the upcoming presidential election, Arizona Senator Barry M. Goldwater, for agreeing with him that the resolution was necessary. Johnson had shrewdly solicited Goldwater's support before he addressed the nation.

Johnson, who was running against the hawkish Goldwater as a "peace candidate," ended his address with the conviction "that firmness in the right is indispensable today for peace." He simultaneously assured

President Johnson faced the difficult decision of how to best respond to reported attacks on American vessels in the Gulf of Tonkin. *(Courtesy of the Lyndon Baines Johnson Library. Photo by Yoichi R. Okamoto.)*

the public he would always be cautious in his use of military force. "Its mission is peace," he explained.

President Johnson took six minutes to inform the citizens of the United States that they now faced a far greater commitment to the war in Vietnam than ever before. After the resolution was passed, the official role of the United States would shift from advising and supplying war goods to South Vietnam to becoming an active participant in the war against the Communist insurgents of North Vietnam and their supporters in the south. In a matter of months, the United States would take almost total control of the war. According to the president, two unprovoked attacks on two different U.S. destroyers in the international waters of the Gulf of Tonkin made this strategic shift in policy necessary.

Although several members of Johnson's administration insisted he did not need congressional approval to send American troops into direct action, Johnson chose to send a resolution to Congress. Johnson was too smart a politician to take such a controversial step without the political backing of the U.S. Congress. He was not going to take full responsibility for the decision.

The passage of the resolution—officially titled Senate Resolution 189, but better known as the Gulf of Tonkin Resolution or the Tonkin Gulf Resolution—was rushed through Congress in two days and received almost unanimous support. It marked the official point of no return for America's involvement in the most bitterly divisive, and ultimately unsuccessful, armed conflict in American history. During the next eleven years, until South Vietnam finally collapsed before the North Vietnamese army in 1975, the Vietnam War would shatter U.S. consensus on foreign policy; divide Americans along generational, political, and racial lines; cost billions of dollars; and end the lives of over fifty-eight thousand Americans and an estimated three million Vietnamese.

"Slipped into the quagmire" is a phrase often used to describe U.S. entrance into the war, giving the image of a huge nation stumbling into its first military defeat. There are some, however, who do not think the United States simply slipped into war. They think politicians and military commanders secretly decided to lead the country into the war, and they also argue these leaders waited for the most opportune time to announce their decision to send American troops to fight in Vietnam.

No matter which of these views one takes, the events of the Tonkin Gulf affair remain unclear and controversial to this day. Historians and military and political analysts continue to speculate about a number of murky points surrounding the landmark incident: What really happened in the Gulf of Tonkin on the second and the fourth of August 1964? Did the resolution Congress passed reflect the president's true intentions? Was the resolution equivalent to a declaration of war, granting President Johnson—and later President Richard M. Nixon—a free hand to conduct an unlimited offensive war in Southeast Asia? If so, did the representatives who voted for the resolution understand they were vesting the president with such a sweeping war power authority? Finally, what is the legacy of the events of August 1964? What lessons does this legacy hold for present-day Americans facing a dangerous world?

This book explores the historical events that preceded American involvement in Vietnam before turning to the two nights in early August 1964 that would forever change the country's course of action. The details of the Tonkin Gulf affair come from the most reliable eyewitness reports and official U.S. correspondence. In the end, it is up to the reader to make up his or her own mind about the controversial events surrounding America's official entry into the Vietnam War.

Chapter Two

Defeat of the French

The events of August 1964 were the result of nearly twenty years of American involvement in Vietnam and other parts of Southeast Asia. At the end of World War II, successive presidents and advisors made a series of decisions that slowly, but inexorably, drew the United States into a dominant role in the conflict between the Communists of North Vietnam and the western-supported government in South Vietnam. As with everything else about the conflict, the story is complicated.

Prior to World War II, France controlled Vietnam, Laos, and Cambodia, which had formed a valuable part of its colonial empire since the 1860s. Near the end of World War II, France intended to reclaim its colonial possessions in Southeast Asia. President Franklin D. Roosevelt and President Harry S. Truman, who succeeded Roosevelt in April 1945, agreed not to interfere in the area if the French promised to work toward eventual independence for the countries.

Vietnam was under French colonial rule from the mid-1800s until World War II. The Mekong River, which runs south from China through Southeast Asia, forms a delta in South Vietnam. *(Courtesy of the Library of Congress.)*

France offered vague promises of allowing national self-determination for its former colonies in Southeast Asia, but it soon discovered promises were not enough. The French leaders underestimated the determination of the former colonies to govern themselves. Not only in Southeast Asia but all over the world, formerly colonized peoples were determined to throw off the yoke of western governments. The French and American leaders were not alone in failing to realize how drastically the attitudes of many of their colonial subjects had changed during the war. The British were making the same discovery in India, Burma, and Malaya. People in the colonies were no longer willing to submit to imperial rule. The Vietnamese and others in "French Indochina" did not want even a temporary return to the former colonial order.

French officers conducting manuevers in Vietnamese rice paddies in 1939.
(Courtesy of the Library of Congress.)

An indigenous army in Vietnam, centered in the north of the country and commanded by a leader who called himself Ho Chi Minh, had fought against Japanese occupation forces during World War II. Before the war, Ho Chi Minh, whose birth name was Nguyen Sinh Cung, had lived in France and other parts of the West. He had begun his political life as a nationalist, a patriot who simply wanted France to leave his country. When he realized none of the western countries with democratic governments were going to support a free Vietnam, he became a member of the French Communist Party. In the years before World War II, the Communists advocated the end of western control of less developed countries.

At the end of World War II, Ho Chi Minh refused to disband his army and allow Vietnam to peacefully return to colonial servitude. On September 2, 1945, the day of Japan's formal surrender to American General Douglas MacArthur aboard the U.S. battleship *Missouri*, Ho Chi Minh and his compatriots announced the establishment of the Democratic Republic of Vietnam (DRV). The seat of the new government was the city of Hanoi, in the north.

France had no intention of turning the country over to the new regime in Hanoi, and President Truman supported France's position. At the time, Truman was more interested in having France's support for a military alliance of European nations and the United States to serve as a bulwark against Soviet expansion in Europe. The alliance became the North Atlantic Treaty Organization (NATO). Truman did not want to risk angering the French over what he saw as a relatively less significant problem in Southeast Asia. He later signaled his approval of France's plans to remain in the area

Communist leader Ho Chi Minh wanted independence from colonial rule for Vietnam. *(Courtesy of the Library of Congress.)*

by extending U.S. diplomatic recognition and offering military aid to the states of Indochina "associated" with France, which included Vietnam, Laos, and Cambodia. These acts mark the beginning of the U.S. involvement in Vietnam.

Before the French moved to reclaim control in early 1946, Ho Chi Minh had already achieved near total political power. He offered the French a peaceful compromise that Vietnam would exist within a vague "French union." Negotiations broke down in September 1946. By December, the two sides were in a war that would last for eight years.

What historians now refer to as the First Indochina War ended when Ho Chi Minh's Vietminh (a contraction of *Vietnam Doc Lap Dong Minh*, or League for Vietnamese Independence) forces besieged French troops at Dien Bien Phu in May 1954. At the time of the French defeat, and France's subsequent withdrawal from a war that had become bitterly unpopular at home, the United States was paying for eighty percent of France's war costs—nearly three billion dollars between 1950 and 1954. The flood of American dollars in support of the French was seen, in Washington, to be part of the U.S. policy of containment.

The concept of containment, which was the long-term strategic policy pursued by the United States at the time to "contain" the spread of the Soviet Union's sphere of influence and the ideology of communism, had originated with George F. Kennan, a diplomat and U.S. State Department advisor on Soviet affairs. In an

President Harry S. Truman *(left)* shakes hands with General Douglas MacArthur in 1950. *(Courtesy of the Harry S. Truman Presidential Library.)*

article entitled "The Sources of Soviet Conduct," published in the quarterly *Foreign Affairs* in July 1947, Kennan proposed a "long-term, patient but firm and vigilant containment of Russian expansive tendencies." He hoped such a policy would endure until the Soviet regime either mellowed or collapsed from within.

The United States first tested the containment policy in March 1947, when it offered immediate economic and military aid to Greece and Turkey after Soviet-supported indigenous Communists threatened both countries with attack. In asking Congress for four hundred million dollars to send to the region, President Truman declared that henceforth "it must be the policy of the United States to support free peoples who are resisting attempted subjugation by armed minorities or outside pressures." This policy soon became known as the Truman Doctrine.

This doctrine was also implicit in America's most successful postwar venture, the European Recovery Program—popularly known as the Marshall Plan after its chief designer, Secretary of State George C. Marshall. Under Marshall's direction, the U.S. sent thirteen billion dollars into Western Europe over five years, restoring economic vitality and confidence to the region, while undermining the local Communist Parties.

In 1948, when the Soviets blockaded the Western-occupied zones of Berlin, the Truman Doctrine again came into play. The United States and Britain supplied these zones by dropping shipments from the air until the Soviets called off their blockade ten months later. Also, in 1949, as a logical outgrowth of U.S. policy, European and North American nations united to form NATO, in opposition to the Soviet dominated Warsaw Pact that controlled most of Eastern Europe.

The containment policy that worked well in Europe was less successful in Asia. President Truman sent George Marshall to China in 1946 to attempt to negotiate an end to the civil war between the Communist forces of Mao Tse-tung and the Nationalist armies of Chiang Kai-shek. The Communists had been decimating the Nationalist forces on the battlefield, as well as doing a better job of winning popular support. This presented Marshall with a nearly impossible task. The Communists knew Chiang was on the ropes and saw no reason to stop fighting when victory was at hand. Despite Marshall's best efforts, his mission failed. Mao defeated Chiang in 1949 and forced the Chinese Nationalists to flee to the island of Taiwan, 115 miles off the Chinese mainland.

On Taiwan, the Nationalist regime declared itself the legitimate government of China. Although it could not win on the battlefield, the Nationalists were more successful garnering the support of many U.S. politicians and business executives who loosely organized into a group dubbed the "China Lobby." Its members included such notable figures as Senators William F. Knowland, Kenneth Wherry, and Styles Bridges, House Majority Leader Joseph W. Martin, and *Time* and *Life* magazine publisher Henry R. Luce. The China Lobby relentlessly attacked the Truman administration for not providing more support to the Nationalists. They insisted this failure resulted in the "loss of China." In the early 1950s, the China Lobby's super-heated rhetoric, which even hinted that China had fallen because of a Communist conspiracy within the Department of State, helped create the so-called "red scare." They provided material for the investigations of the red scare's most prominent figure, Senator Joseph R. McCarthy, who made a career of accusing American officials, as well as artists, writers and actors, of secretly being Communists.

By the end of 1949, Mao's forces had conquered all of mainland China and reached the borders of Vietnam. A major Asian country had fallen to Communism. Only six months later, on June 25, 1950, the Communist forces of North Korean dictator Kim Il Sung surged across the thirty-eighth parallel into American-allied South Korea. The containment policy was again being directly challenged. President Truman rushed U.S. armed forces to South Korea. The focus of America's containment policy had shifted from Europe to Asia.

Chapter Three

Johnson Takes Charge

The war in Korea lasted for three years, from 1950 to 1953. U.S. troops fought along with other forces from the United Nations. During the same years, French troops were slowly losing the war to maintain control of Vietnam. As the situation worsened, the French government called on the U.S. for more help. During the last decisive battle at Dien Bien Phu, French leaders appealed to President Dwight D. Eisenhower, who had succeeded President Truman, to intervene militarily. Eisenhower said he could not do so without the support of Congress, something he did little to secure and which he knew would not be forthcoming. He did not want to send American troops into the conflict. Dien Bien Phu fell and the French agreed to leave Vietnam. Ironically, Senator Lyndon B. Johnson adamantly opposed U.S. intervention in Vietnam on the side of the French.

Because President Eisenhower did not provide military support to the French at Dien Bien Phu, he is often seen as having resisted deepening U.S. involvement in Vietnam. Yet Eisenhower's administration supported another fateful decision that led to a deeper U.S. role in what was becoming the Vietnam quagmire.

At the 1954 conference in Geneva that brokered the French withdrawal from Vietnam, U.S. delegates insisted Vietnam be divided into two nations at the seventeenth parallel. As part of the agreement, democratic elections were scheduled to be held within two years. After the country was divided, however, the Eisenhower administration supported South Vietnam's pro-Western leaders when they reneged on their promise. Eisenhower later admitted the decision to forgo the election had been made because "possibly eighty percent of the population would have voted for Ho Chi Minh as their leader."

After France withdrew from Vietnam, the United States assumed the role of the dominant Western power and protector of the Vietnamese against the Communist North. Although U.S. delegates to the Geneva conference had pledged the United States would not intervene militarily in Vietnamese affairs, Eisenhower bluntly announced afterward that the United States "has not itself been party to, or bound by, the decisions taken by the [Geneva] conference." Instead, on October 23, 1955, the United States supported the establishment of a new government for the Republic of Vietnam (RVN or South Vietnam).

During the remainder of the 1950s, the Eisenhower

administration worked to establish and develop the Southeast Asia Treaty Organization (SEATO), which was designed as a bulwark against Communist expansion in the region. The Ho Chi Minh-led government in Hanoi, Democratic Republic of Vietnam, continued to wage a political *dau tranh* (struggle) against South Vietnam. In an effort to disrupt the North Vietnamese, Eisenhower sent covert operatives of the Central Intelligence Agency (CIA) into North Vietnam. The United States also sent several hundred military advisors and over one billion dollars of aid to the South Vietnamese government located in Saigon.

Ngo Dinh Diem controlled the South Vietnamese government. Diem was pro-Western, anti-Communist, and Catholic, while most Vietnamese were Buddhists. Despite U.S. attempts to prop up the Saigon government, it was never able to win widespread popular support. Not only was Diem viewed as too "Western" by many Vietnamese, his administration was also corrupt and did little to improve citizens' lives.

The containment policies begun by the Truman administration continued during the Eisenhower years. The new president coined a descriptive metaphor for the policy during a press conference on April 7, 1954. While explaining the strategic importance of Southeast Asia, he said: "You have a row of dominoes, and you knock over the first one, and what will happen to the last one is the certainty that it will go over very quickly." Thereafter, the containment policy earned the nickname of the "domino theory."

In the same press conference, Eisenhower went on to say he feared the Republic of South Vietnam might become the first "domino" to topple. He stopped short of saying that, should the Saigon government collapse, whatever U.S. political party in power at the time would pay a price, as had happened after the Nationalists lost in China. Because of the reaction to the Communist victory in China, American politicians were becoming unwilling to risk appearing to be "soft on Communism," particularly in Asia. This fear would play a big role in the decisions that were made, by both Democrats and Republicans, in the years leading up to 1964.

In January 1959, North Vietnam's decision-making body, or Politburo, issued Resolution 15 stating its policy toward South Vietnam was changing from a "political struggle" (*dau tranh chinh tri*) to an "armed struggle" (*dau tranh vu trang*). The adoption of Resolution 15, which was essentially a declaration of war by the North Vietnamese, marks the official beginning of the Second Indochina War, more popularly known in the United States as the Vietnam War. The following May, the Fifteenth Plenum (general assembly) of the North Vietnamese Communist Central Committee formally sanctioned Resolution 15 and notified their allies in the South, the National Front for the Liberation of Vietnam, known to American soldiers as the Vietcong, to commence guerrilla operations against the government in South Vietnam.

The Vietcong (a contraction of *Viet Nam Cong San*, or Vietnamese Communist) were made up of former members of the Vietminh who had remained in South Vietnam, plus new members recruited from the southern population. Hanoi directed the activities of the Vietcong, which were aimed at destabilizing the Saigon government and supplementing the more conventional military operations of the regular North Vietnamese Army.

In 1960, Eisenhower assured South Vietnamese President Diem, "The United States will continue to assist South Vietnam in the difficult yet hopeful struggle ahead." Eisenhower, who would be leaving office in January 1961, hoped his promise would bind future presidents to his policies.

President John F. Kennedy, Eisenhower's successor, began expanding the U.S. military presence in Vietnam soon after taking office. When President Kennedy was a senator from Massachusetts, he called South Vietnam "the cornerstone of the Free World in Southeast Asia" and "a test of American responsibility and determination." Throughout his 1,037 days in the White House, Kennedy vigorously pressed ahead on the course of deepening the intervention already charted by his predecessors. Kennedy was determined his administration would not be accused of allowing the spread of Communism in Asia.

Several members of the Kennedy administration would play crucial roles in U.S. policy in Vietnam for the next eight years, including Vice President Johnson, Secretary of State Dean Rusk, and National Security Advisor McGeorge Bundy. No member of the Kennedy administration, however, would wield more influence on U.S. policy in Vietnam—excluding Presidents Johnson and future president Richard M. Nixon—than Secretary of Defense Robert S. McNamara.

McNamara, who had served as president of Ford Motor Company for two months before Kennedy picked him to come to Washington, had been a surprise choice. Kennedy wanted someone from the corporate world to run the Department of Defense. He thought a business executive, skilled in new management theories, would streamline the vast Defense Department bureaucracy and invigorate it with improved methods of operation. No one in the corporate world came more highly rec-

Secretary of Defense Robert S. McNamara would play a crucial role in the escalation of the Vietnam War in both the Kennedy and Johnson administrations. *(Courtesy of the Lyndon Baines Johnson Library. Photo by Yoichi R. Okamoto.)*

ommended than McNamara, whose peers generally regarded him as brilliant. His youth and expertise with systems analysis and other recently developed management tools made him one of the shining stars of the new administration.

Kennedy and his advisors continued Eisenhower's hard line on Communism, but they questioned his reliance on massive nuclear retaliation as a deterrent to Communist aggression. Eisenhower thought the fear of U.S. nuclear superiority would frighten enemies and save the U.S. from having to spend billions on more conventional forces. Kennedy considered this nuclear dependence too limiting. As an alternative, McNamara and General Maxwell D. Taylor, chairman of the Joint Chiefs of Staff, developed a new strategy combining the use of diplomacy, covert (secret) action, counterinsurgency (anti-guerilla) operations, and conventional forces. Taylor explained having a variety of options would enable the United States to respond "anywhere, at anytime, with weapons and forces appropriate to the situation."

These options came at a high cost. To enable the United States to respond to nonnuclear aggressions with sufficient conventional forces, the Kennedy administration doubled the number of ships in the navy and increased the size of the army from eleven to sixteen divisions. It also expanded the number of tactical air squadrons from sixteen in 1961 to twenty-three by the mid-1960s, while increasing U.S. airlift capacity by seventy-five percent. To help thwart Communist guer-

President Kennedy *(right),* Secretary of Defense Robert McNamara *(center),* and General Maxwell Taylor *(left),* attempted to develop a strategy to fight Communist guerrillas in Vietnam. *(Courtesy of the Library of Congress.)*

rillas worldwide, Kennedy approved the creation of a new counterinsurgency force—the Green Berets—whose name he personally selected.

In 1961, Kennedy established a fifteen-member Special Group, directed by General Taylor, for the express purpose of coordinating U.S. counterinsurgency activities around the globe, particularly in Southeast Asia and Latin America. By June 1963, thousands of U.S. military officers, as well as at least seven thousand from foreign countries allied with the United States, had undergone counterinsurgency training at the Army's

Special Forces School at Fort Bragg, North Carolina.

When Kennedy took office, he thought the United States lacked sufficient armed forces to defend Western Europe—its first priority—let alone South Vietnam. Consequently, he decided the South Vietnamese should be trained to fight their own war on the ground. He planned to use the Green Berets to train and aid the Army of the Republic of Vietnam (ARVN). His goal was to train the South Vietnamese and then, hopefully, remove most of his advisors. In the meantime, the number of advisors steadily increased from nine hundred in 1961 to about 16,300 by November 1963.

On February 8, 1962, the United States established the U.S. Military Assistance Command Vietnam (MACV) in Saigon to supervise the advisors and the other support personnel ordered to South Vietnam by President

American military personnel trained the South Vietnamese army during the years preceding the Tonkin Gulf affair. *(AP Photo.)*

The hamlet program was designed to keep citizens safe from Vietcong attacks, yet many resented the forced relocations and abandoned the hamlets after President Diem was killed. *(AP Photo.)*

Kennedy. This pattern of gradually increasing troop levels and command structure would be repeated more than once over the next years.

Through 1962, the ARVN, assisted by the Green Berets, experienced some success against the Vietcong. At the same time, South Vietnamese President Diem initiated his strategic hamlet program, designed to separate and protect the peasantry from the Vietcong guerillas. The program, aided by the Americans, was also intended to win the "hearts and minds" of the people and work as a political extension of the military effort. For a time, it enjoyed moderate success.

By autumn of 1963, it had become clear to the Kennedy administration that the Diem regime was a disaster. One reason for Diem's failure was corruption, of which there were many reports. American reporters in Saigon wrote stories of how the bulk of U.S. aid was spent on building up a police organization designed more to keep the South Vietnamese citizens under control than to stop the Vietcong. The rest was spent on the military and very little went toward fostering economic development. This inability, or refusal, to address the social and economic needs of the people left them more receptive to the arguments of the Communists, who were promising a society based on economic equality. There were also charges that Diem was so afraid of a coup against him, he spent most of his time and money creating military units to protect himself against his rivals in the South Vietnamese military. In short, Diem appeared more concerned with maintaining power than fighting the Communists.

Diem's fear of a coup was well founded. He had angered many important South Vietnamese leaders by

Ngo Dinh Diem, shown casting a ballot in 1961, was the president of South Vietnam until he died in a military-led coup in November 1963. *(Courtesy of Library of Congress.)*

Diem's sister-in-law, Madame Nhu, was highly critical of Buddhism, the religion of most Vietnamese people. *(AP Photo.)*

keeping governmental control within the grasp of his family. Diem installed his brother Ngo Dinh Nhu as chief political officer and head of the secret police. Other family members held dictatorial control over various South Vietnamese provinces. Diem rejected requests from his American benefactors to make internal political reforms. Inevitably, unrest and dissent began to surface among his citizenry.

The final stage of the political crisis that led to Diem's downfall began when his brother violently broke up a Buddhist peace demonstration in May 1963. Because the Ngo family was Catholic, a faith often viewed as a remnant of French colonialism by the more nationalistic Vietnamese in both the North and the South, this action alienated the Buddhist majority. Nevertheless, Diem and his brother continued to brutally disperse several more Buddhist demonstrations. Diem's sister-in-law, a militant Catholic, seemed to take personal delight in ridiculing the Buddhists. In protest of the regime, several Buddhist monks set fire to themselves, but Diem, despite warnings from the U.S., refused to stop his brother's brutal suppression of dissidents.

In late August 1963, Nhu's police forces in Saigon, Hue, and other cities, arrested many Buddhists. This sparked widespread protest among the South Vietnamese people and aroused grave concerns in Washington about the stability of Diem's regime.

After Nhu's crackdowns, Washington and Saigon exchanged a complex series of communications regarding the increasingly explosive situation. Patience was running thin among administration officials. They wor-

Several Buddhist monks immolated themselves in protest of the persecution of Buddhists under Diem. *(Courtesy of the Library of Congress.)*

ried Nhu's oppressions were adversely affecting the containment effort. Three days after the arrests, U.S. Undersecretary of State George Ball cabled U.S. Ambassador to Saigon Henry Cabot Lodge and instructed him to "urgently examine all possible alternate leadership and make detailed plans how we might bring about Diem's replacement if this should become necessary."

Ball's instructions suggest the Kennedy administration was preparing for—if not orchestrating—a military overthrow of the Diem regime. Kennedy, his top security advisors, and Ambassador Lodge all agreed Diem posed a major threat to American policy objectives in Vietnam, but they could not agree how to resolve the Diem dilemma. This eventually led to a decision to "not thwart" a coup, should one arise. Skeptics find it hard to believe that Kennedy failed to realize Diem's enemies among the South Vietnamese army officers would interpret this "neutral" position toward a coup as a signal to move forward with their plans to seize power. Essentially, the Americans were saying they would no longer protect the leadership they had supported for almost a decade.

On November 1, 1963, South Vietnamese officers, led by Major General Duong Van Minh, launched their coup. Diem and his brother Nhu surrendered to them the next day and were promptly executed. General Minh seized control of the South Vietnamese government.

Once again, U.S. officials had helped to shape internal policy in South Vietnam, while avoiding taking a public stance. Their fingerprints were nowhere to be

Diem's assassination led to rioting in the streets of Saigon. *(Courtesy of the Library of Congress.)*

found, although they did not disagree with the outcome. The United States was still avoiding taking public positions on internal Vietnamese affairs. This was one of the policies that would come to an end with the passage of the Tonkin Gulf Resolution.

Word of the political assassinations in Saigon shook President Kennedy's confidence in U.S. policy in Vietnam. He had little time, however, to reevaluate whether to move forward in Vietnam or to withdraw from what was beginning to look like a no-win situation. Three weeks after the murder of Diem and his brother, an assassin's bullets brought down President Kennedy.

After Kennedy was killed in Dallas, Texas, Vice President Lyndon B. Johnson became president on November 22, 1963. In assuming the highest office in the land, Johnson also took charge of the deepening American involvement in Vietnam. His decisions over the next few months would culminate in the Gulf of Tonkin Resolution—and in the long years of war that followed.

Chapter Four

Covert Maritime Operations

No one can say with certainty what policy John F. Kennedy might have followed in Vietnam, but none of his actions up to the time of his death dissuaded Lyndon B. Johnson from continuing to expand America's presence in Vietnam. President Johnson retained most of Kennedy's top foreign policy advisors—Secretary of Defense Robert McNamara, Secretary of State Dean Rusk, General Maxwell Taylor, National Security Advisor McGeorge Bundy, and others. Not surprisingly, the Johnson administration remained committed to Kennedy's flexible response doctrine, with particular emphasis on covert operations.

On December 12, 1963, McNamara informed Ambassador Lodge that President Johnson wanted to see proposals and plans for increased secret operations against North Vietnam. McNamara wrote:

Covert operations by South Vietnamese forces, uti-

After the assassination of President John F. Kennedy, Vice President Lyndon Baines Johnson was sworn into office aboard Air Force One. *(Courtesy of the Lyndon Baines Johnson Library.)*

lizing such support of U.S. forces as is necessary, against North Vietnam. Plans for such operations should include varying levels of pressure all designed to make clear to the North Vietnamese that the U.S. will not accept a Communist victory in South Vietnam and that we will escalate the conflict to whatever level is required to insure their defeat.

On December 15, 1963, two groups—the MACV and

the CIA—jointly proposed a modified version of an earlier Pacific Command plan. The new plan, designated OPLAN 34A, called for four categories of operations against the North. These ranged in severity from minor nuisance activities, such as "small unspectacular raids," up to "aerial attacks conducted against critical DRV [North Vietnamese] installations or facilities, industrial and/or military, such as POL [petroleum, oil, and lubricants] storage areas, thermal power and steel plants, the loss of which would result in crippling effect on the DRV potential to maintain a stable economy and progress in industrial development." The plan called for South Vietnamese forces to carry out these attacks without the direct involvement of U.S. forces.

The stated aim of the final version of OPLAN 34A was to act "in concert with other military and diplomatic actions in the Southeast Asia area, to convince the DRV leadership that its current support and direction of war in the Republic of Vietnam . . . should be reexamined and stopped." The drafters of the plan, however, did not offer any assurances it would succeed.

In retrospect, the plan reveals the Americans were unrealistic in assessing the effectiveness of covert operations. The underlying premise that covert operations would convince the North Vietnamese the United States stood ready "to escalate the conflict to whatever level is required" was never examined critically. Furthermore, the South Vietnamese forces had never demonstrated the ability to carry out consistently successful air attacks against North Vietnam.

In hindsight, OPLAN 34A suggests a level of wishful thinking on the part of American policy makers. It was becoming clear the South Vietnamese could not win the war without direct, offensive American military help. Today, the plan seems like a last-ditch attempt to avoid full U.S. involvement.

Robert McNamara signed off on OPLAN 34A in December 1963, and President Johnson approved it on January 16, 1964. Marine Corps Major General Victor Krulak, a counterinsurgency specialist working for the Joint Chiefs of Staff in Washington, selected some of the plan's less risky options and drafted a twelve-month schedule of implementation. Krulak's schedule specified three phases of increasing intensity. Phase I would commence in February and last through May 1964.

On January 24, 1964, the Johnson administration established the Special Operations Group (SOG), which was placed under the MACV. SOG was responsible for covert raids against the North. (The group was later given the less-revealing title of "Studies and Observations Group.") During the 1950s and early 1960s, the CIA conducted covert activities aided by the military. With the formation of SOG, these roles reversed. The military would now conduct covert operations with the assistance of the CIA.

While the U.S. military reorganization in South Vietnam was evolving, the political situation in Saigon continued to deteriorate. The removal of Diem had not led to a more stable government. Before General Duong Van Minh could consolidate his power, he was deposed in a bloodless countercoup led by another major general, Nguyen Khanh. General Khanh had justified the coup to Ambassador Lodge by claiming Minh had failed "to respond to the exigencies of the struggle against communism." He appointed himself prime minister and vowed to "fight communism to the final victory."

In Hanoi, Ho Chi Minh, witnessing the political turmoil in Saigon, decided the time had come to launch the next stage of insurgency, which called for the infiltration of regular North Vietnamese army units into South Vietnam to assist the Vietcong's guerrilla actions. This more conventional military invasion would require a substantial increase in the flow of supplies from North to South Vietnam. The Gulf of Tonkin and the South China Sea—which provided many points of entry along

In 1964, General Nguyen Khanh launched a successful coup against U.S.-supported General Minh. *(Courtesy of the National Archives.)*

the long and lightly guarded coast of South Vietnam—offered the best route for supplying both the Vietcong and the regular army. This decision led to direct conflict with the United States.

As early as 1961, in their own attempt to take advantage of the porous nature of South Vietnam's mostly unguarded coastline, the CIA initiated the implementation of covert maritime operations, or marops, to help stem the flow of supplies to the Vietcong from the North. Marops, the agency was convinced, would also discourage Hanoi from provoking insurrection in the South. To direct its marops program, the CIA selected Tucker Gougelmann, a tough former marine who had served in the South Pacific in World War II, and in Korea, Afghanistan, and Eastern Europe in the 1950s.

In the summer of 1961, Gougelmann set up a base in Da Nang, South Vietnam, just south of the seventeenth parallel, and began running boats north. Commandos of South Vietnam's First Observation Group carried out the covert raids under the code name Nautilus. The commandos were conveyed to their targeted destinations, inserted, and extracted by junks, or flat bottom boats. Hanoi responded to the commando raids by building a navy capable of defending its coastline.

On January 8, 1962, the U.S. Navy commissioned its own special warfare units—SEAL Team One at Coronado, California, and SEAL Team Two at Little Creek, Virginia. The teams drew their acronym from the first letters of the elements by which they infiltrate, operate, and disengage—*SE*a-*A*ir-*L*and.

In Vietnam, the SEALs would later operate in highly secret intelligence missions for the navy's River Patrol Forces and as part of MACVSOG. They required an armed, high-speed, shallow-draft (depth) boat capable of operating in hostile coastal waters and inserting, supporting, and extracting a SEAL team.

Later in 1962, Washington directed the CIA to start "harassment and short-term sabotage raids . . . as a limited response to the escalation of North-South hostilities and as preparation for the future establishment of resistance activity within North Vietnam." But Gougelmann's tiny fleet of small craft consisted of little more than South Vietnamese motorized junks. These lumbering vessels were simply not fast or agile enough to meet the stealth and speed requirements necessary to carry out harassment and sabotage operations. Washington, recognizing the limits of Gougelmann's fleet, authorized him to be supplied with advanced naval support and equipment.

Also, in August 1962, General Paul D. Harkins, the first commander of MACV, "proposed the use of U.S. motor torpedo boats, supported by a naval logistic [supplies and services] unit based in Da Nang, for runs to the north." The Kennedy administration approved Harkins's request the following month, and the navy examined its inventory for suitable craft. In October, the navy reactivated two mothballed, aluminum-hulled torpedo boats and designated them PTF-1 and PTF-2 (PTF stands for Patrol Type, Fast). The PTFs experienced repeated malfunctions during sea trials, however.

A navy captain reported to Secretary of Defense McNamara the boats were not suitable and had been deactivated.

Despite problems with the PTFs, McNamara saw their reactivation as "a step in the right direction." He thought more should be done to convince Hanoi it would pay a stiff price for continuing to foment insurrection in South Vietnam. As his next step, McNamara requested "priority attention also be given to the procurement of foreign-made craft." He then directed the secretary of the navy to "take immediate action to procure two boats of the Norwegian Navy's Nasty class."

The eighty-eight-foot mahogany-hulled Norwegian Tjeld (Nasty) Class torpedo boat was light and heavily armed, usually with twin .50-caliber machine guns and an 81mm mortar. It was designed for high-speed, short-range defense of national waters. Two diesel engines powered it to burst speeds of forty-seven knots. (A knot, or nautical mile, is equivalent to 1.151 land miles per hour.) About a third as wide as it was long, the Nasty

Norway supplied the United States with Nasty class torpedo boats in Vietnam. *(Courtesy of the U.S. Naval Historical Center. Collection of Admiral Arleigh A. Burke, USN.)*

had a low silhouette and was difficult to detect with radar. The navy procured two Nasties in December 1962 and designated them PTF-3 and PTF-4. They were shipped to the Far East in the fall of 1963, for use in Vietnam. A half dozen more Nasties would join them by the following June.

Supplementing the Nasties and the South Vietnamese junks, numerous American-built Swift boats were assigned to MACVSOG marops. The twin-screwed, aluminum-hulled Swift boat—designated PCF (Patrol Craft, Fast)—had an overall length of fifty feet and a width of thirteen and a half feet. Powered by two diesel engines, the Swift reached a top speed of twenty-eight knots. Although smaller and slower than the Nasty, it carried similar armaments and was often confused with the Norwegian-built craft in reported sightings.

Following the transfer of responsibility for covert operations that commenced in November 1963 and culminated with the creation of the SOG on January 24, 1964, Secretary of Defense McNamara insisted the first raid under OPLAN 34A take place by February 1—only one week later. The secretary wanted to "make it clear to the leaders of the North that they would suffer serious reprisals for their continuing support of the insurgency in South Vietnam." At this time, McNamara wanted to send a symbolic message to Hanoi and thus limited targets to "those that provide maximum pressure with minimum risk."

Upon its inception, SOG subdivided itself into several sections according to the nature of its operations.

The Maritime Operations Group and SOG's first forward operating base were established at Da Nang. An Air Studies Group, another group of advisors, was sent to Nha Trang. The marops group operated out of Da Nang under the cover name of Naval Advisory Detachment, or NAD. Other SOG subdivisions included its psychological warfare section and two ground operations groups—Northern Infiltrations and Cross-border Operations.

To accommodate McNamara's demand for immediate activity, the Air Studies Group launched an air mission on February 1, 1964. Maritime operations did not commence until February 16. In one of the not infrequent oddities of warfare, the first marop conducted by NAD against a North Vietnamese objective utilized Norwegian captains to pilot American-built Swifts carrying South Vietnamese commandos.

Washington insisted on maintaining plausible deniability for any involvement in acts of war against North Vietnam. Accordingly, the rules of engagement for maritime operations strictly prohibited the use of U.S. personnel, but training the inexperienced South Vietnamese sailors to use the new powerboats proved to be difficult. This problem prompted the CIA to recruit the Norwegians in July 1963 to skipper some of the high-speed craft. Although U.S. Navy SEALs provided training for the South Vietnamese raiding parties, SEALs were not allowed to take part in any raids.

On the night of February 16, 1964, three Norwegian-piloted Swifts departed their base at My Khe, just outside Da Nang, and raced north with a team from the South Vietnamese *Lien Doi Nguoi Nhai* (LDNN), literally, "frogman unit." The mission was to blow up a Soviet-built Swatow patrol craft, gunboats that formed the backbone of the North Vietnamese navy, at Quang Khe, as well as a ferry at Cap Ron. The raiders, however, were caught swimming upriver toward their targets and the mission failed. Two subsequent attacks on Quang Khe in March also failed. The participating frogmen in all three raids were either killed or captured.

In early April, barely two months after the implementation of OPLAN 34A had officially begun, Admiral Harry D. Felt issued a progress report to the Joint Chiefs of Staff in Washington. As commander-in-chief in the Pacific, Felt commanded all U.S. military forces in Vietnam. The admiral noted, "Five attempts to infiltrate teams by sea on sabotage missions had failed." The first successful maritime operation did not come until May. By then, President Johnson and his advisors were already drafting plans to escalate the war in Vietnam.

Chapter Five

Planning Ahead

Lyndon B. Johnson became president with only one year remaining until the next presidential election. As he met the worsening situation in Vietnam, he considered how every move he made would affect his chances of winning an election on his own to the office he had wanted his entire life.

Johnson was aware of his place in history and had been a participant in many of the decisions of the recent past. He had been in Washington, D.C., as an aide, representative, or senator since the 1930s. He remembered how the conservative wing in the Republican Party accused the Truman administration of "losing China" following the Communist takeover in 1949. Johnson knew America's ability to influence, much less control, events in other countries was limited, and the charge against Truman was unfair. Nevertheless, he thought the Nationalist defeat in China would always be a black mark against Truman. Early in his presidency,

Johnson remarked privately, "I am not going to lose Vietnam. I am not going to be the president who saw Southeast Asia go the way China went."

If the United States were to abandon Vietnam, he warned later, "it might as well give up everywhere else—pull out of Berlin, Japan, South America." Johnson might have added that to show softness in the face of Communist advances in South Vietnam could cost him the election.

In December 1963, the Joint Chiefs of Staff began formulating a series of tough options for responding to Hanoi's transgressions in the South. (Created during World War II, the Joint Chiefs of Staff represent the various branches of the military and coordinate the strategies of the U.S. armed forces.) The chiefs planned to submit the options formally to the new president in January. According to the chiefs, a U.S. defeat in its confrontation with Communism in South Vietnam would deal a blow to their reputation for "durability, resolution and trustworthiness" throughout Asia. An American loss would also undermine "our image" in Africa and South America. The chiefs adhered to the domino theory and were preparing to suggest "increasingly bolder" U.S. measures in Vietnam. Word of its plans spread quickly through official circles in Washington.

The suggestions of the Joint Chiefs included U.S.-South Vietnamese air strikes and commando actions against North Vietnam and intelligence flights over Cambodia and Laos. If necessary, they favored the introduction of regular U.S. combat forces. Most of all, in their view, it was essential that a U.S. commander take charge of "the actual direction of the war." The Joint Chiefs of Staff were ready to turn the struggle in Vietnam into an American war. Johnson did not initially agree with their recommendation to deepen U.S. involvement in Vietnam, but he would come to accept many of their suggestions over the next months. He understood he could not appear "soft on Communism."

At a White House reception on Christmas Eve, Johnson told the Joint Chiefs of Staff, "Just get me elected, and then you can have your war." Whether he meant to keep that promise—or whether he meant it as a promise at all—is not clear. What is clear is that Johnson did get elected, and the Joint Chiefs did have their war.

Johnson would have preferred to focus on his plans for a Great Society, particularly the "war on poverty" and the advancement of civil rights for African Americans and others who had been denied full citizenship for centuries. He inherited the American involvement in Vietnam. He certainly wanted to win the 1964 election, and that factored into his decisions. McNamara and his military advisors also persuaded him that the best policy in Vietnam was to escalate the conflict, openly involve U.S. forces, and quickly bring it to a close. His goal was probably the sort of negotiated settlement that had ended the open fighting in Korea. By the end of the summer of 1964, he was convinced that this goal could be attained in a matter of months, if not weeks.

Johnson wanted to control when the United States became more deeply, and publicly, involved in this unpredictable war on the other side of the globe. In the months immediately after the Kennedy assassination, he worked to keep the "brushfire" war from blazing out of control. He approved covert rather than overt operations to keep Vietnam out of the headlines, while preparing to step up the war if it became necessary—and at a time of his own choosing.

The first covert actions under OPLAN 34A commenced on February 1, 1964. At a meeting in the White House on February 20, President Johnson directed: "Contingency planning for pressures against North Vietnam should be speeded up. Particular attention should be given to shaping such pressures so as to produce the maximum credible deterrent effect of Hanoi." Planning for bombing targets in North Vietnam and for carrying out other military "contingencies" started at once and continued over the next year.

Planners of military operations usually rely heavily on intelligence data. OPLAN 34A operations provided one means of acquiring such data. To help with the gathering of information, the Joint Chiefs of Staff authorized the resumption of DeSoto patrols in the Gulf of Tonkin in January 1964. "DeSoto differed substantially in purpose and procedure from 34A operations," writes Robert McNamara in his memoirs. "They were part of a system of global electronic reconnaissance carried out by specially equipped U.S. naval vessels. Operating in international waters, these vessels collected radio and radar signals emanating from shore-based stations on the periphery of Communist countries such as the Soviet Union, China, North Korea, and, more to the point here, North Vietnam."

The DeSoto patrols began in 1962. When they resumed in the Gulf of Tonkin in 1964, the U.S. destroyer *Craig* carried out the first patrol. It departed from Keelung, Taiwan, on February 25. Its main purpose was to collect information on North Vietnamese coastal defenses that might prove useful to future OPLAN 34A raids.

Although both the DeSoto patrols and the 34A raids were conducted in the same waters during the same time, they operated independently of one another and were under separate commands. Pacific Fleet commander Admiral Thomas H. Moorer determined the frequency and course of DeSoto patrols, subject to the approval of the Joint Chiefs; SOG directed OPLAN 34A operations. In fact, in an effort to maintain this distinction, planners of the *Craig*'s cruise were careful to ensure that no 34A raids were scheduled during the time of the destroyer's patrol. This distinction played a role in the events leading up to the clash of U.S. and North Vietnamese naval vessels in the Gulf of Tonkin in early August.

The United States did not want to provoke China. The *Craig* was directed to stay offshore of all Chinese islands by at least twelve miles. By comparison, they were given permission to come within four miles of any North Vietnamese islands. Bad weather during the cruise impeded visual observance but did not hamper electronic data gathering.

The *Craig* carried a "communications van" that contained radio receivers for monitoring local radio communications and a staff of analysts to interpret them. It also carried an electronic countermeasures (ECM) van and a staff of analysts. The *Craig* had more radar-detecting equipment than a destroyer normally carries. The North Vietnamese, suspicious of the ship's activities, shut down all its signal-emitting equipment along the coast, and the *Craig*'s communications and ECM analysts experienced a boring cruise. The patrol gathered little intelligence of value.

On March 6, 1964, Secretary McNamara and General Maxwell Taylor, the chairman of the Joint Chiefs, flew to Saigon to evaluate the effectiveness of the initial covert operations and to assess the stability of the new government of South Vietnamese Premier Khanh. They did not like what they saw.

McNamara later wrote about the covert operations: "Long before the August events in the Tonkin Gulf, many of us who knew about the 34A operations had concluded they were essentially worthless. Most of the South Vietnamese agents sent into North Vietnam were either captured or killed, and the seaborne attacks amounted to little more than pinpricks." (Pinprick was a term frequently used by appraisers of OPLAN 34A actions to define their effectiveness.) Covert operations were allowed to continue, according to the defense secretary, only because "the South Vietnamese saw them as a relatively low-cost means of harassing North Vietnam in retaliation for Hanoi's support of the Vietcong."

McNamara was no more optimistic about the political situation in South Vietnam. When he returned to Washington, McNamara candidly reported to the president: "The situation has unquestionably been growing worse, at least since September 1963." His memorandum stressed three major problems:

> 1. In terms of government control of the countryside, about 40 percent of the territory is under Vietcong control or predominant influence. In twenty-two of the forty-three provinces the Vietcong control 50 percent or more of the land area.
> 2. Large groups of the population are now showing signs of apathy.
> 3. In the last ninety days the weakening of the government's position has been particularly noticeable.

His memo went on to suggest new U.S. objectives in Southeast Asia. Up till then, official U.S. policy had been to help the South Vietnamese "win their contest against the externally directed and supported Communist conspiracy." In his memo, which President Johnson approved and reissued the next day as National Security Action Memorandum (NSAM) 288, McNamara now proposed an enlargement of this limited objective in two areas.

First, NSAM 288 stated: "We seek an independent non-Communist South Vietnam . . . South Vietnam must be free . . . to accept outside assistance as required to maintain its security." In other words, as a recognized nation, South Vietnam had the right to request U.S. assistance in its fight against the North. This redefinition of U.S. objectives would provide the foundation of American policy toward South Vietnam for the next five years.

Second, the NSAM expanded U.S. aims throughout Southeast Asia: "Unless we can achieve this objective in South Vietnam almost all of Southeast Asia will probably fall under Communist dominance . . . Thus, purely in terms of foreign policy, the stakes are high." The Johnson administration had now formally adopted the domino theory that had been the working policy in Asia since the Eisenhower administration.

Backed by the full weight of the presidency and the National Security Council, NSAM 288 is an important milestone on the path to the complete United States commitment to saving South Vietnam. On the day of its issuance, President Johnson ordered an increase of sixty million dollars in U.S. aid to South Vietnam, and promised Premier Khanh that the United States would finance a fifty-thousand-man increase in the South Vietnamese army and supply it with new equipment. Johnson also promised funds for modernizing governmental systems and administrative processes.

Although McNamara's memo described the worsening situation in South Vietnam in strong terms and prescribed a drastic enlargement of U.S. objectives throughout Southeast Asia, he recommended only a limited number of actions.

Lieutenant General Phillip B. Davidson, who served as intelligence officer under two MACV commanders in Vietnam, offers a partial explanation for the disparity between the secretary's proposal to broaden U.S. aims in Asia and the scarcity of specific suggestions. Referencing a memorandum draft from Assistant Secretary of Defense William P. Bundy to the president, dated March 1, 1964, Davidson writes, "The broadened objectives of McNamara's memo are a direct lift from Bundy's memo, but where Bundy [an advocate of congressional approval for further action in Vietnam] had logically recommended aggressive action against North Vietnam—a blockade of Haiphong [a key seaport near Hanoi], followed by United States air strikes in the North—McNamara proposed a much more restrained program."

McNamara opposed bombing North Vietnam at the time, but he said the United States should begin preparing for future air attacks should they become necessary. Acting on McNamara's proposal, President Johnson directed the Joint Chiefs to start planning retaliatory air strikes against North Vietnam that could be launched in seventy-two hours. In response, the Joint Chiefs of Staff directed Admiral Harry D. Felt to draft a more detailed contingency plan—Operations Plan 37-64—that the Joint Chiefs approved in April.

Similar to NSAM 288, OPLAN 37-64 covered potential U.S. actions in Laos, Cambodia, and South Vietnam, as well as in North Vietnam. After its initial approval, refinements analyzed targets in North Vietnam, including the type and scale of attack required to yield specific degrees of damage. The resulting compilation eventually grew into what became known as the "94 Target List."

The National Security Council Executive Committee met on May 24 and 25, with the Johnson administration now thinking seriously about striking at North Vietnam soon. The meeting ended with the committee recommending a firm presidential decision on attacking North Vietnam at some unspecified date in the future. They assumed the situation in South Vietnam would not improve enough "to make military action in North Vietnam unnecessary." The committee hoped American preparations would be enough of a threat to persuade Hanoi to remove its forces from South Vietnam.

On May 25, working from a memorandum from two days earlier, the State Department produced a draft of a congressional resolution approving past military actions in Vietnam and authorizing the administration to take all future actions necessary to stop the Communist aggression. The president's national security advisors debated the need for a resolution into June. They finally agreed to ask for a congressional resolution authorizing "wider action" in Vietnam before the administration unleashed a military campaign against the North.

The lengthy State Department draft declared, "The

United States regards the preservation of the independence and integrity of the nations of South Viet Nam . . . as vital to its national interest and to world peace." The clause authorizing military action carried the main thrust of the proposed resolution:

> To this end, if the President determines the necessity thereof, the United States is prepared, upon the request of the Government of South Viet Nam . . . to use all measures, including the commitment of armed forces to assist that government in the defense of its independence and territorial integrity against aggression or subversion, supported, controlled or directed from any Communist country.

After the resolution was revised one more time, it was ready to be sent to Congress. They just needed the right timing. Most senior officials concurred an appeal for the resolution should be put off until later in the year so as not to stir up a "war fever" in Congress. At a June 10 meeting, however, Secretary McNamara echoed the opinions shared by the top officials when he suggested, "in the event of a dramatic event in Southeast Asia we would go promptly for a Congressional resolution."

President Johnson decided to wait patiently for the right moment to present the resolution authorizing widening the U.S. effort in Vietnam. It would be eight weeks before television newscasts featured the events in the Gulf of Tonkin, but when it happened the "Tonkin Gulf" resolution was ready and waiting.

Chapter Six

Troubled Waters

In late May 1964, while President Johnson and his advisors in Washington were planning how best to escalate U.S. actions, South Vietnamese commandos carried out the first successful covert maritime operation under OPLAN 34A. Two Nasty boats had recently been delivered to the Naval Advisory Detachment (NAD) in Da Nang. The NAD fleet now comprised two gas-fueled torpedo boats called "gassers," two Nasties, and three Swift boats. With the contracts of the highly regarded Norwegian sailors scheduled to expire in mid-June, SOG decided to use their expertise on one final operation that would be the baptism by fire for the Nasties.

The operation involved snatching the crews off of North Vietnamese fishing junks and whisking them to Cu Lao Cham, a small island about fourteen miles offshore of Da Nang. On Cu Lao Cham—code-named "Paradise Island"—the crews would be tricked into believing an anti-Communist resistance movement was

American soldiers land helicopters loaded with supplies for the South Vietnamese in 1964. *(Courtesy of the Library of Congress.)*

operating in their midst within North Vietnam. The deceived fishermen would then be returned to North Vietnam to spread the word about the movement. The first "kidnapping" mission was deemed a success and others followed.

Buoyed by their first success, NAD planners entered Phase II of OPLAN 34A from June through September with renewed optimism. Although the Norwegians departed in June, NAD compensated by acquiring eight Nationalist Chinese skippers from Taiwan. These boats were better suited for abduction operations. Had a captured fisherman sighted a white-faced Norwegian on one of these missions, the deception would probably not have worked.

The Nasties excited SOG. They moved faster than the Swifts and their greater range extended SOG's strike capability to the entire North Vietnamese coast, while the Swifts had only allowed movement as far as southern Ha Tinh province. The Nasties could also transport three times as many raiders. Moreover, they could outrun anything in North Vietnam's navy. Coastal missions now began producing a measure of success.

On June 12, NAD tested the full potential of a newly arrived Nasty by targeting a coastal depot in the Ky Anh district of Ha Tinh province. Arriving offshore of Ky Anh, twenty-six members of the Biet Hai (or "sea commandos") of the South Vietnamese navy slipped into three rubber boats powered by muffled outboard motors and sped for shore. Once landed, they crossed the beach and assaulted a combination storage facility and barracks. For ten minutes, they raked their target with machine-gun fire and 57mm recoilless-rifle rounds. They took no return fire. Leaving the facility aflame, all twenty-six commandos returned safely to the Nasty.

SOG followed this success with another cross-beach raid, this time against the Hang Bridge on Route 1—a main highway that roughly followed the coastline of Vietnam. Previously, NAD planners had avoided scheduling raids in times of a full moon, preferring less illumination for their stealth attacks. Emboldened by their recent success, however, NAD scheduled this attack for the night of a full moon. The gamble paid off.

Thirty-one Biet Hai sped to their distant target in a new Nasty boat. Seven commandos, covered by the other two dozen, blew up the bridge. Backtracking toward their beached rubber boats, the raiders encountered a four-man North Vietnamese patrol and killed them all. They returned safely to the Nasty without losing a man. It was another success.

From Saigon, Ambassador Lodge, always pessimistic about the chances of democracy succeeding in South Vietnam, had reported earlier to the White House that OPLAN 34A missions "might be good training but were certainly having no effect on Hanoi." Lodge was not the only critic of covert operations against the North. High-level military leaders also disapproved of them.

Admiral Harry D. Felt, commander in chief of the Pacific, had never favored covert marops as an alternative to overt military action. As he neared the end of his tour as the Pacific naval chief, Felt observed, "lack of adequate intelligence is a prime factor in the failure of maritime operations." He also saw the North Vietnamese buildup of Chinese-built Swatows plus Hanoi's "increased state of alert and mobilization" as additional obstacles. Admiral Felt, who strongly advocated U.S. intervention in Vietnam, concluded, "The odds against pulling successful operations under present conditions are high."

Pacific Fleet commander Admiral Ulysses S.G. Sharp, shared Felt's assessment of covert ops. "I have been watching this program closely," Sharp wrote, "and see . . . some of our early reservations on the PTF concept becoming reality." He also noted Hanoi's vigilance was "more extensive and effective than originally thought."

Meanwhile, in Washington, Joint Chiefs of Staff Chairman Maxwell Taylor expressed the group's concerns about the strategy. "While we are wholly in favor of executing the covert actions against North Vietnam," the chairman wrote, "it would be idle to conclude that these efforts will have a decisive effect." Even Defense Secretary Robert S. McNamara, OPLAN 34A's principal proponent, began to doubt its effectiveness. He eventually admitted, "This program will not amount to very much." Despite the unspectacular achievements of covert ops in Phase I, OPLAN 34A missions continued. The marginal successes even prompted Washington to ask SOG to increase operations against North Vietnamese coastal defenses—specifically, to initiate actions that "embodied destruction of greater scope and intensity involving targets of greater criticality than those in Phase I."

Washington was raising the stakes in the Far East, at the same time as changes were taking place in U.S. leadership personnel in the Pacific and in South Vietnam. Ambassador Henry Cabot Lodge resigned in May, and the White House named the multilingual Joint Chiefs of Staff Chairman Maxwell Taylor to replace him in July. On June 20, deputy MACV commander Lieutenant General William C. Westmoreland, who had held many important posts in the army, replaced MACV commander General Paul D. Harkins, who had lost the support of the Johnson administration. Ten days later, Admiral Ulysses S.G. Sharp, a hard-line proponent of escalating the war in Vietnam, succeeded the retiring

In the summer of 1964, General Maxwell Taylor *(right)* replaced Lodge as ambassador and General William Westmoreland *(left)* became MACV commander. *(Courtesy of the Library of Congress.)*

Admiral Harry D. Felt as top naval commander in the Pacific. Within a period of weeks, there were three new U.S. leaders in place.

In Da Nang, NAD now threw caution to the sea breezes. Marops planners reasoned they could make their raids more effective by sending two Nasties on the next mission—one to carry the commandos, and a second to serve as escort. They planned to return to Dong Hoi to target a pumping station near the water reservoir north of town. At midnight June 30, again under a bright moon, two Nasties closed in on Dong Hoi, near the mouth of the Kien River. While one of the boats stood by, the other Nasty offloaded rubber boats and thirty Biet Hai jumped in. Muffled outboards sprang to life, and the commandos raced shoreward.

As a reaction to NAD's earlier raids, Hanoi had placed its coastal security forces on heightened alert. A hail of tracer fire greeted the commandos when they landed on the beach. Some of the raiders returned fire, while others hauled three 57mm recoilless rifles within sight of the pumping station and fired off eighteen rounds. The intense North Vietnamese fire forced the attackers to flee back to the beach, leaving the recoilless rifles behind. The two Nasties drew in close to shore and joined the firefight with their deck guns. Twenty-eight raiders made it back to the boats safely. Two did not.

In 1964, Marine Lieutenant Colonel James Munson served as NAD's deputy chief for operations. He planned NAD's maritime operations and understood better than anyone the abilities and limitations of the Biet Hai. Although some thirty-two marops were scheduled between April and December 1964, Munson was not impressed with their results: "I would note that most of the missions launched never made it, they aborted and came back. Those that did not abort were destructive, but it seemed like a mighty small pinprick." The "pinpricks" continued into July, as NAD also launched psychological warfare operations against North Vietnamese naval bases at Quang Khe and Ben Thuy.

On July 15, Nasty-borne NAD commandos struck again near Cap Ron—this time on a moonless night. The darkness did not work to their advantage, however. Alerted North Vietnamese coastal defenders met the raiders on the beach and forced them to abort the attack. The commandos again lost two men.

Although the raids were intensified over the early summer of 1964, they were not of any major consequence. The war was still not going well in the South.

The strength and effectiveness of the Vietcong in the countryside seemed to be growing. The hope was that the covert operations would, by pinpricking the North, let the leaders in Hanoi know they would soon be paying a price for their aggression.

Following the failed attack at Cap Ron, NAD planners canceled a scheduled operation against Vinh Son when intelligence sources reported increased patrol activity by the North Vietnamese navy in the area. SOG then proposed an increase in maritime operations against the North Vietnamese coastline, but suggested bombarding installations from offshore rather than inserting commandos. In Saigon, new MACV commander General William C. Westmoreland approved of the plan, and SOG began training South Vietnamese raiders to use 81mm mortars, 4.5-inch rockets, and recoilless rifles from aboard the boats. On July 30, Westmoreland revised the 34A marops schedule for the month of August. He nearly tripled the scheduled number of raids.

On that same night—although there were reports of increased enemy patrol activity—four PTF boats churned out of their base at Da Nang and headed north to bombard naval installations on the North Vietnamese islands of Hon Me and Hon Ngu. The U.S. destroyer *Maddox* had left port at Keelung, Taiwan, two days earlier. Unknown to SOG, the destroyer was embarking on another DeSoto patrol and would soon draw close to the North Vietnamese coastline. The waters of the Gulf of Tonkin were becoming dangerously congested.

Chapter Seven

The First Sign of Trouble

It is ironic that a war fought primarily on land was sparked by events that happened at sea. The events precipitating the most divisive war in American history, however, are still clouded in controversy. Those events began unfolding in July, 1964.

In Saigon, General Westmoreland requested naval assistance to help gather intelligence about North Vietnamese coastal defenses in the areas where new OPLAN 34A raids were to be conducted. A week later, apparently in response to the request, Admiral Ulysses S.G. Sharp scheduled another DeSoto patrol along the North Vietnamese coastline for the end of July. Sharp assigned the patrol to the U.S. destroyer *Maddox*, which was captained by Commander Herbert Ogier. For this patrol, however, Captain John J. Herrick, a seasoned commander of the Seventh Fleet's Destroyer Division 192, was to sail aboard the *Maddox* and assume command of the mission.

On July 26, the *Maddox* arrived at Keelung, Taiwan, the home base for DeSoto operations. It tied up against the destroyer *MacKenzie* to take aboard a communications van. Its officers instructed Captain Herrick and the officers of the *Maddox* on the procedures unique to DeSoto patrols.

The communication van (comvan)—basically a shipping container loaded with radio equipment—was the only one in the Pacific area. It was operated by fifteen specialists, handpicked by Lieutenant Gerrill Moore, the assistant operations officer of the Naval Security Group Activity based in Taiwan. While on a DeSoto patrol, comvan specialists worked in two shifts, twelve hours on and twelve hours off.

The USS *Maddox* patrolled the Vietnamese coastline in the waters of the Tonkin Gulf.
(Courtesy of the Library of Congress.)

Captain Herrick *(left)* and Commander Ogier of the USS *Maddox*. *(Courtesy of the U.S. Naval Historical Center.)*

The comvan did not contain state-of-the-art electronic surveillance gear. To the contrary, as Lieutenant Moore later explained, it "had been built on a shoestring budget—primarily using equipment discarded by other operating facilities." Its radio listening gear "was standard radio equipment used on Navy ships all over the world on a day-to-day basis. (The old reliable R-390 radio receiver, in fact, was our primary intercept equipment)."

An on-line teleprinter was the *Maddox*'s only piece of high-tech equipment. It enabled the destroyer to receive and transmit information intercepted by the shore-based stations. The teleprinter could quickly decrypt and print out messages of concern, which would be immediately delivered toto Captain Herrick.

Although the comvan did not contain any electronic countermeasures (ECM), two ECM specialists formed a part of Lieutenant Moore's team. Working alongside the destroyer's regular radar operators, rather than in the van, their expertise lent a greater sophistication to the analyses of intercepted North Vietnamese radar signals than could be expected of ordinary radarmen. Their ECM skills were otherwise inappropriate to the requirements of the *Maddox's* upcoming DeSoto patrol.

The *Maddox*, not equipped for high-tech intelligence gathering, relied on more conventional surveillance methods—visual observation, photography, and the use of the ship's radar to locate and chart onshore radar stations. Water temperatures and depths were sounded and recorded using an instrument called a bathythermograph.

Captain Herrick and the officers of the *Maddox* received a final briefing on July 27. No one came away with a sense of how important their mission would become. Gerrill Moore recalls looking forward to a "leisure cruise." A directive from Vice Admiral Roy L. Johnson, the new Seventh Fleet commander, did caution that the destroyer should regard any unusual scrutiny by North Vietnamese patrol craft, aircraft, or radar installations as "a significant event."

On July 28, the *Maddox* slipped its moorings in Keelung and put to sea, charting a course for the South China Sea. The destroyer's itinerary called for it to rendezvous with the U.S. oiler *Ashtabula*, due east of the seventeenth parallel, for underway refueling on July 31. It would then sail to sixteen distinct points along the coast of North Vietnam. Its intelligence-gathering mission would begin at the seventeenth parallel and continue north to the Chinese border. The ship would stop and circle at checkpoints, picking up electronic signals before moving on.

Two nights later, while the *Maddox* was still en route to its refueling rendezvous, four fast boats left Da Nang and headed north. When they reached the demilitarized zone that straddled the seventeenth parallel, they turned out to sea to distance themselves from the hostile shoreline. About five hours later, just before midnight on July 30, they drew close to their objectives—the offshore islands of Hon Me and Hon Ngu.

The four boats waited until they were within striking distance of the islands before cutting their engines. Although the crews could not see their targets in the dark night, they knew Hon Me lay to the northwest and Hon Ngu to the southwest. They quietly reviewed their plans and paired off. Lieutenant Son, one of the finest boat captains in the covert fleet, led the attack at Hon Me with two boats, while Lieutenant Huyet commanded the attack at Hon Ngu with the other two. Lieutenant Son's Nasties commenced their run to shore at twenty minutes after midnight, July 31.

Speeding shoreward, the raiders could see their target silhouetted in the darkness—a water tower rising high out of a cluster of military buildings. Suddenly, before they reached the beach, North Vietnamese machine guns opened fire. Bullets riddled one boat, ripping away part of its bow and wounding four crewmen, including Lieutenant Son. Moments later, another crewman shouted a chilling warning—a North Vietnamese Swatow patrol boat was bearing down on them.

The raiders scrapped all plans for going ashore to plant demolition charges. They would have to rely on their deck guns to inflict as much damage as possible on their target. Staying their course in the face of withering gunfire, the boats dashed toward shore. Illuminated in the harsh glare of North Vietnamese flares that hung in the night sky, the Nasties poured 20mm and 40mm fire and 57mm recoilless rifle rounds into their target. The attack lasted less than twenty-five minutes before the Nasties broke away and streaked for home. They arrived safely back at Da Nang before noon.

The sight of the damaged boat's shattered bow caused a few raised eyebrows among the NAD advisors at Da Nang. "The whole port bow from the water-tight panel just below the bridge was shot up," recalled Lieutenant James Hawes, a SEAL training officer. "I'm surprised it made it back." Worse yet, Lieutenant Son died after his arm was shredded from elbow to fingers by fragments from a 14.5mm round. "We were sad to see him go," said Hawes. "He was a gutsy guy." Nevertheless, the raid was considered to be a success.

At Hon Ngu, Lieutenant Huyet's boats motored to within eight hundred yards northeast of the island undetected. Shortly after midnight, the two boats crept close enough to shore for the crews to see their target— a communications tower—in the moonlight. Both boats opened fire, raking the tower and then turning their fire on to other nearby structures. The attack caught the defenders completely by surprise. They met only scant resistance from ineffective North Vietnamese machine-gun fire. Huyet's raiders kept up their attack for forty-five minutes, then headed for home.

The raids against Hon Me and Hon Ngu drew the South Vietnamese raiders so far north they were closer to Haiphong than to Da Nang. SOG headquarters applauded the operation, calling it "well executed and highly successful, with secondary explosions."

Meanwhile, in the early morning of July 31, while the PTFs were speeding southward toward Da Nang, the *Maddox* was steaming westward toward the Vietnamese coast on an almost exact line with the seventeenth parallel. At 0629 (Military time uses a twenty-four-hour clock, with midnight represented by 2400, 1:15 A.M. by 0115, 1:00 P.M. by 1300, and so on), the *Maddox* began a partial and selective breaking of radar and radio silence. At 0741, after the *Maddox* had completed its refueling rendezvous with the *Ashtabula*, the first two PTFs passed about four miles ahead of the destroyer on a southerly course. Within the next half hour, the second pair of PTFs passed astern of the *Maddox*, also heading south.

Ostensibly, the separate commands of the 34A operations and the DeSoto patrols did not coordinate the PTF raids on Hon Me and Hon Ngu to coincide with the intelligence-gathering patrol of the *Maddox*. However, Admiral Johnson later revealed that officers of the Seventh Fleet and the MACV had "discussed in detail" the communication links that could be used by MACV to reach the *Maddox* "if 'quick reaction' tie-in with special ops required." This suggests a plan existed to summon help from the *Maddox* if any of the PTFs needed assistance.

After the PTFs had passed by, the *Maddox* continued toward the coast for another fifteen miles before fully activating its radar and other electronic equipment and steaming northward to the first of its sixteen listening points. It is not known for certain if the North Vietnamese started tracking the *Maddox* when it selectively lifted its radar and radio silence as they neared the PTFs. If they did, Hanoi could have concluded the destroyer had been purposely stationed at the seventeenth parallel to intercept any North Vietnamese gunboats in hot pursuit of the PTFs. In other words, a U.S. ship was providing military support to the South Vietnamese.

The *Maddox* arrived at Point Alpha at 1320 and spent the afternoon and early evening circling in a listening orbit between Tiger Island (Hon Co) and the North Vietnamese mainland. Tiger Island lies just north of the seventeenth parallel, fifteen miles off the mainland. The ship's orders limited its approaches to no closer than eight miles to the mainland or four miles to islands. This meant its orbit was restricted to about three miles. At 2100, the *Maddox* passed slightly less than four miles from Tiger Island, the closest it would come to North Vietnamese territory during the entire patrol. Before leaving for Point Bravo, Moore's comvan crew detected Communist early warning emissions emanating from this station.

The next morning, August 1, the *Maddox* remained in the vicinity of Point Bravo. It kept eight to twenty miles off the mainland and no closer than four and a half miles to the island of Hon Mat, just east of Hon

Ngu. Captain Herrick, a prudent commander, exerted every effort to keep the *Maddox*'s patrol from becoming unduly provocative to the North Vietnamese. He issued precise gunnery orders: "Do not permit the guns to be trained or elevated at all while under visual observation of an air or surface contact unless specifically authorized by the commanding officer." Given the mood of Hanoi after seven SOG air and sea attacks on its installations in three days (from July 31 to August 2), it is likely the North Vietnamese coastal defense forces considered the *Maddox* to be an even greater threat.

That afternoon, the comvan began detecting evidence that North Vietnamese shore stations were tracking the *Maddox* by radar. The shore defenses showed no signs of being overly disturbed by the destroyer's presence. Steaming north again, the ship sighted a few fishing junks but reported no incidents. It arrived at Point Charlie at 1800 and reached a position five miles south of Ho Vat, an islet off Hon Me, at 2115. All remained calm. The first sign of trouble did not come until the early morning hours of August 2, 1964.

Chapter Eight

The First Incident: The *Real* Encounter

Early on August 2, 1964, the *Maddox* intercepted a message indicating the North Vietnamese navy planned to attack somewhere that night. An officer who saw the message described it as short, no more than a single sentence. It did not identify the intended target. Captain Herrick was awakened to read the message.

In the meantime, at the North Vietnamese Northern Fleet headquarters at Van Hoa (Port Wallut) near the Chinese border, three Soviet-built P-4 torpedo boats and two Swatow gunboats put to sea and headed south to shore up defenses at Hon Me. The eighty-ton Swatows were under-armed with 37mm cannon, light weapons barely adequate for engaging PTFs, let alone destroyers.

Of the vessels available to the North Vietnamese navy, the P-4s stood the best chance in a battle against a destroyer. But since Hanoi apparently was convinced the PTFs would join the *Maddox* and attack the coast of

North Vietnam, the Swatows' 37mm guns were to be used against the PTFs.

The twenty-four-ton, aluminum-hulled, Soviet built P-4 measured about sixty-six feet in length and twelve feet across and could reach a maximum speed of fifty-two knots. It carried two torpedoes with warheads containing 550 pounds of high explosives, plus a pair of 14.5mm machine guns with an effective range of roughly 2,187 yards. The three southbound P-4s were scheduled to arrive at Hon Me at about 0400.

Back aboard the *Maddox*, the comvan team intercepted a second message specifying the location of the "enemy" vessel to be attacked. The location matched that of the *Maddox*. This intercept represented something far more serious than a routine tracking report from a North Vietnamese coastal station. "It came from a higher authority and gave a specific location," Gerrill Moore recalled later, "rather than the range and bearing from an observation post." Putting the first and second messages together, the officers of the *Maddox* concluded their ship was the target. A subsequent third message removed all doubt.

At 0324, Captain Herrick received an American intelligence message warning of imminent danger. Soon afterward, Herrick ordered the *Maddox* out to sea. He wanted to avoid a night-time confrontation. The *Maddox* went to "general quarters" status—combat readiness with all personnel at battle stations. Herrick planned to stay farther at sea until daylight made it safer to move in closer to the coastline.

At 0645, Herrick reported to Admiral Johnson at Seventh Fleet headquarters that the *Maddox* would proceed back toward the coast and head for Point Delta unless otherwise directed. He added, "If info received concerning hostile intent by DRV is accurate consider continuance of patrol presents unacceptable risk." Herrick's orders had cautioned him against taking any "unacceptable risk." The veteran captain understood the grave consequences that might arise from a confrontation between a U.S. destroyer and warships of the North Vietnamese navy. Admiral Johnson took note of Herrick's concern but ordered him to resume the DeSoto patrol.

The *Maddox* arrived in the vicinity of Point Delta at about 1045 and turned south on the first leg of an intended eight-hour orbit off Thanh Hoa province. At 1115, Herrick reported: "Approx 75 junks in area. No other craft visible. Will deviate from track as necessary to avoid passing through junk concentration." The *Maddox* adjusted course and Herrick radioed: "No further evidence of hostile intent."

At the same time, Admiral Johnson and Admiral Sharp received new intelligence indicating the North Vietnamese were stiffening their defenses on Hon Me against further 34A attacks and might attack the *Maddox*. Around 1235, lookouts and radar on the *Maddox* identified three P-4s about ten miles north of Hon Me, traveling southward at twenty knots. Reversing course, the *Maddox* headed northeast toward Point Delta. Soon afterward, the destroyer's lookouts sighted two Swatows north of the island, heading south at ten to fifteen knots. All five North Vietnamese boats put into a small cove on Hon Me. At 1400, they received orders to launch a torpedo attack against the *Maddox*.

By 1500, the *Maddox* was steaming about twelve miles east of Point Delta under overcast skies. Visibility extended to some ten miles, and the sea remained nearly calm in a ten-knot wind. The ship's radar picked up a blip at this time, thirty miles southwest near Hon Me. Operators tracked it and soon identified the contact as a patrol boat because of its thirty-knot speed. The boat held steady on a fifty-degree course, a bearing that paralleled the *Maddox*'s course.

During the next forty-five minutes, the *Maddox* took evasive actions, increasing speed from ten to twenty-five knots and heading east briefly. When more North Vietnamese boats were identified, the destroyer turned abruptly to the southeast. Ideally, for a P-4 to stand any chance at all against a destroyer, it would need to mount a frontal attack. A head-on attack would present a smaller target and allow it to move faster. When the *Maddox* turned to the southeast, however, the P-4s continued on a course that was obviously plotted to intercept the destroyer before it had turned to the southeast. By the time the torpedo boats corrected course, they were behind the *Maddox*.

"The PT boats were behind us because we had already started moving away from them as a result of the [intercepted] messages we received," Commander Ogier recounted afterward. "They approached from astern

because that was the only option that we gave them."
Ogier set general quarters and the men of the *Maddox*
prepared to do battle.

At 1540, Captain Herrick radioed an uncrypted message to the Seventh Fleet commanders stating that his
vessel was "being approached by high-speed craft with
apparent intention of torpedo attack. Intend to open
fire if necessary self defense." The task group commander immediately requested that the U.S. carrier
Ticonderoga provide air support.

On July 8, 1964, the Joint Chiefs of Staff had ordered Admiral Sharp to keep an American aircraft carrier stationed off the coast of South Vietnam "to accomplish recon and weather missions and to be prepared to
conduct strikes if required." In complying with the
order, the scrappy admiral also maintained a large-deck
carrier at Yankee Station—an offshore point at roughly
the same latitude as Da Nang. Aircraft from the USS
Ticonderoga—four F-8E Crusaders that were already
airborne—responded to Herrick's call for air support

The USS *Ticonderoga*
provided air support for the
American ships in the Tonkin
Gulf. *(Courtesy of the Naval
Historical Center.)*

The USS *C. Turner Joy* patrolled the Tonkin Gulf with the USS *Maddox*. *(Courtesy of the U.S. Naval Historical Center.)*

from a distance of some 280 miles southeast of the *Maddox*.

At the same time, the U.S. destroyer *C. Turner Joy*, then serving as the forward radar picket (sentry) ship for the carrier task group, received orders to steam toward the *Maddox* at flank (best possible) speed. Help was on the way.

Meanwhile, around 1605, the three North Vietnamese P-4s closed to about ninety-eight hundred yards astern of the *Maddox*'s starboard quarter (right-hand stern side). By this time, the American destroyer was about twenty-eight miles off the North Vietnamese coast, well outside the twelve-mile limit. The hostile torpedo boats continued to close in fast. They made no attempt—using signal flags, lights, radio, or other means—to communicate with the *Maddox*.

Commander Ogier requested permission from Captain Herrick to open fire on the North Vietnamese attackers. Herrick assented. Later he said he meant the firing to be warning shots not aimed directly at the torpedo boats, and three or four warning shots fell harmlessly, either ahead or in back of the onrushing boats. Undeterred, the P-4s kept on coming. Around 1608, the *Maddox* commenced rapid fire at a range of some nine thousand yards, using a standard mix of explosive shells. The *Maddox*'s five-inch guns had a range of eighteen thousand yards.

Initially, the three torpedo boats closed in on the *Maddox* from astern in numerical order, with the command vessel (T-333) leading, followed by the other two (T-336 and T-339). The two torpedo tubes on a P-4 were angled outboard about 1.5 degrees, and the boat captain usually fired both torpedoes with a single push of the firing lever. The North Vietnamese attack procedure called for the three boats to fire their torpedoes at about the same time, from a range of six hundred to one thousand yards. Using angled tubes and simultaneous firings, the attackers hoped to spread the torpedoes far enough apart that the targeted ship would find it difficult to avoid taking at least one hit.

Their tactics failed them when the lead boat (T-333) tried to pass the *Maddox* in order to fire its torpedoes from abeam of the destroyer. Unobserved by the destroyer, the T-336 fired first, launching one of its two torpedoes from between nine thousand and five thousand yards astern. Captain Herrick reported, "Because her torpedo was launched or because of heavy fire from *Maddox*, the lead boat [now the T-336] temporarily turned away to south. 2d and 3d vessels, T-339 and T-333, continued to attack."

The T-339 launched two torpedoes within three thousand yards of the *Maddox*, then took a hit from one of the destroyer's five-inch guns. It turned away from the exchange in clear distress. The *Maddox* changed course to 110 degrees to avoid the T-339's torpedoes, which passed starboard of the destroyer within two hundred yards. The T-333 did not turn toward its target until after the T-336 and the T-339 together had already fired three torpedoes.

At that point, the T-333, with North Vietnamese squadron commander Captain Le Du Khoai on board, passed the *Maddox* without firing its torpedoes. The T-336 rejoined the battle, unleashing its second torpedo and firing its 14.5mm guns at the U.S. warship. A 14.5mm round struck the pedestal of the Mark 56 fire director aboard the *Maddox* and lodged in an ammunition-handling compartment below. Fire from the destroyer raked the T-336 as it passed astern, killing its captain, Lieutenant Nguyen Van Tu.

The attackers then broke off the action and headed for home, ending the surface engagement only twenty-two minutes after it had begun. Commander Ogier said later, the "attacking boats were aggressive and showed no tendency to abort their torpedo run even though they were confronted with a heavy barrage of fire."

In the brief confrontation, the *Maddox* had loosed 283 shells at its attackers—seventy-one five-inch AAC (antiaircraft, common), 132 three-inch VT-frag (variable time, fragmentation), sixty-eight five-inch VT-frag, and twelve five-inch star (illuminated) shells. (The star shells were inappropriate to the action and had been fired mistakenly.) The air attack had yet to begin.

Captain Herrick ordered the *Maddox* to pursue the fleeing attackers. When it became clear the slower destroyer could not catch the high-speed torpedo boats, he called off the chase. Shortly thereafter, the four F-8E Crusaders from the *Ticonderoga* appeared overhead. Herrick, fearing the *Maddox* might hit unexploded torpedoes in the area, opted to let the planes handle the P-4s. He directed them toward the enemy boats, then informed his superiors he intended to leave the Gulf of Tonkin "at best speed." The *Maddox* steamed out of harm's way to the southeast.

The Crusaders, led by Commander James B. Stockdale, caught up with the fleeing P-4s and pounced on them. Stockdale and junior grade Lieutenant Richard Hastings attacked the two lead boats—the T-333 and T-336—while Commander R.F. Mohrhardt and Commander C.E. Southwick attacked all three boats. All four aircraft launched Zuni rockets and strafed with 20mm cannon. A hit by a Zuni would have been clearly visible, but none of the pilots saw evidence that any of the rockets had made contact. Although Hanoi later reported a rocket had hit one boat, an after-action report filed from the carrier stated that "the Zunis did not hit the targets."

Twenty-millimeter cannon fire proved more effective than rocketry against the P-4s. American pilots scored hits on all three torpedo boats, hitting the T-339 the hardest. The Crusader pilots left the T-339 dead in the water and later reported it sunk. Crews of the other two boats, unable either to locate the T-339 or to contact it by radio, also reported that it had been lost in action.

Hastings reported to his flight mates he had suffered wing damage from hostile gunfire. Stockdale, who saw the damage, attributed it to stress on the wing of the F-8 when Hastings had pulled out of his dive. (The F-8 was known for stressing easily.) In any case, Hastings was forced to make an emergency landing at Da Nang. When a second flight of four Crusaders arrived on the scene, the other three Americans, now running low on fuel, returned to the *Ticonderoga*.

With the *Maddox* out of danger, Seventh Fleet commander Roy L. Johnson took steps to limit the consequences of this brief clash. He ordered the second flight of Crusaders not to pursue the North Vietnamese torpedo boats and no further action was taken. The T-333 and T-336, though damaged, made it back to shore and beached for repairs at the mouth of the Son Ma River. Despite reports of its being lost, the severely damaged T-339 limped to shore on the island of Hon Ne, a few miles north of the estuary. All three boats survived to fight another day.

So ended the first incident—the encounter we are sure took place—between the naval forces of the United States and North Vietnam in the blue waters of the Gulf of Tonkin. A second incident—which might be one of the greatest illusions in the annals of sea fighting—would quickly follow on its heels.

Chapter Nine

The Second Incident: Ghosts in the Gulf

In Washington, D.C., on the morning of August 2, President Lyndon B. Johnson met with his senior advisors. It was nineteen hours after the first incident in the Gulf of Tonkin. (Washington time is twelve hours behind Vietnam. It was 11:30 P.M. in the Gulf of Tonkin.) The president wanted to review the latest reports and consider a U.S. response to the attack on the *Maddox*. Eventually, they decided on a restrained reaction.

"The group believed it was possible that a local North Vietnamese commander—rather than a senior official—had taken the initiative," Secretary of Defense Robert S. McNamara wrote later, "and the president therefore decided not to retaliate. He agreed instead to send a stiff protest note to Hanoi and to continue the [DeSoto] patrol, adding another destroyer, the *C. Turner Joy*."

McNamara went on to point out that Maxwell Taylor, now the U.S. ambassador in Saigon, opposed the decision not to retaliate. In a late-night cable to the State Department on August 2, Taylor expressed concerns that the lack of a U.S. response to an attack on an American warship in international waters would be construed as an "indication that the U.S. flinches from direct confrontation with the North Vietnamese."

That same night, the president met with CIA Director John McCone at the White House. McCone, once an uncompromising advocate of massive retaliation, now opposed escalating the war in Vietnam. Johnson asked him, "Do they want a war by attacking our ships in the middle of the Gulf of Tonkin?" McCone did not think so. He felt convinced Hanoi was instead reacting to the SOG raids on Hon Me and Hon Ngu. "The North Vietnamese are reacting defensively to our attacks on their offshore islands," he said. "The attack is a signal to us that the North Vietnamese have the will and determination to continue the war." Although the United States officially denied any connection between the DeSoto patrols and the covert maritime operations conducted against North Vietnam by the South Vietnamese, it is easy to see how Hanoi would consider them to be linked.

Secretary of State Dean Rusk saw no need to reassure Hanoi it was not a joint mission. He indicated his delight that Hanoi was shaken and later notified the Saigon embassy that even larger commando raids were planned for the near future. Rusk, a holdover from the Kennedy years, had become one of President Johnson's favored advisors. In the troubled times ahead, the secretary would steadfastly back the president's position and repeatedly support Pentagon requests for ever-greater troop commitments in South Vietnam, as well as the bombing of North Vietnam.

Secretary of State Dean Rusk. *(Courtesy of the Lyndon Baines Johnson Library. Photo by Yoichi R. Okamoto.)*

While Johnson pondered North Vietnam's intentions, regiments of Communist soldiers were winding down the so-called Ho Chi Minh Trail—a network of roads and paths stretching from North Vietnam through Laos into South Vietnam. This transportation system was the main supply route for troops and material sent to support the Vietcong and North Vietnamese troops in the South. Hanoi was steadfastly committed to reunifying Vietnam and was building up supplies and troops in Laos and elsewhere. This buildup and planning was much more significant to the Communists than a few small boat raids and a couple of destroyers cruising off the coast of North Vietnam. In retrospect, it seems clear that U.S. officials overvalued the importance of their covert actions at sea, and the marops continued.

On the afternoon of August 3, 1964, four boats—PTFs-1 and -2 (the American-made patrol boats) and PTFs-5 and -6 (Nasty boats) cleared their berths in Da Nang and headed north. Each boat carried a sixteen-man crew and was armed with a 57mm recoilless rifle and machine guns. This time, they were targeting a North Vietnamese radar installation at Vinh Son and a security post on the banks of the nearby Ron River. Both targets were about ninety miles away. PTF-2 experienced engine trouble and was forced to turn back. The remaining three boats sped on and rendezvoused off the coast from Vinh Son.

Racing shoreward, PTFs-1 and -5 commenced their attack on the radar station, pummeling it with fire for twenty-five minutes before turning for home. At the same time, PTF-6 stationed itself at the mouth of the Ron and set the night sky and the enemy security post ablaze with illumination rounds. (The post had been the scene of an earlier, failed, cross-beach raid.) The last Nasty took some return fire but no casualties. A Swatow gunboat gave chase when the PTF-6 headed for home, but the faster Nasty soon outdistanced it. All three boats arrived back at Da Nang shortly after daybreak.

Throughout the previous night, top-level U.S. commanders had been conducting long-distance debates, trying to decide whether the DeSoto patrols should be continued. Captain Herrick favored terminating them, noting: "It is apparent that DRV has cut down the gauntlet and now considers itself at war with the US. It is felt that they will attack US forces on sight with no regard for cost. US ships in the Gulf of Tonkin can no longer assume that they will be considered neutrals exercising the right of free transit."

Vice Admiral Johnson, Seventh Fleet commander, agreed with Herrick, but his immediate superior, Pacific Fleet commander Admiral Thomas H. Moorer, did not. Moorer, aboard the *Ticonderoga*, sent a top priority message to Herrick, stating, "In view [of the] *Maddox* incident consider it in our best interest that we assert right of freedom of the seas and resume Gulf of Tonkin patrol earliest."

Herrick pointed out, "DRV PTs have advantage especially at night of being able to hide in junk concentrations all across the Gulf of Tonkin. This would allow attack from short range with little or no warning . . . Consider resumption of patrol can only be safely undertaken by DD, CL/CA [destroyer, light/heavy cruiser] team and with continuous air cover." In the end, Admiral Sharp agreed with Moorer, and the patrol resumed.

On August 3, the *Maddox*, now accompanied on the patrol by the *C. Turner Joy*, reentered the Gulf of Tonkin and steamed to a position off Thanh Hoa province, near Cape Ron. Herrick retained operational control as commander Task Group 72. No cruisers were available on short notice, but Admiral Moorer ordered aircraft from the carriers *Ticonderoga* and *Constellation* to provide the destroyers with continuous daytime air cover.

Herrick's new orders called for the destroyers to

proceed to Point Charlie, advance to Point Delta, then backtrack to Point Charlie on August 4. They were supposed to remain at least twelve miles off the coast of North Vietnam. Over the following three days, the task group was to steam through other designated points before ending the patrol. Both destroyers were to retire to the relative safety of the central gulf at the close of daylight hours.

The *Maddox* and the *C. Turner Joy* arrived at Point Delta at about 1400 on August 4, 1964, and then began backtracking toward Point Charlie, with aircraft from the *Ticonderoga* circling overhead. At 1435, Captain Herrick reported having been shadowed from a distance of about fifteen miles by a vessel he tentatively identified as a motor gunboat. By then, the destroyers had intercepted several North Vietnamese radio messages. One message identified the American vessels, a second ordered motor gunboats to prepare for night operations, and two intercepts spoke of action with the U.S. ships. The Americans, alert to the potential danger, spent much of the day at general quarters.

The task group arrived at a point northeast of Point Charlie at 1700, changed course to due east, and headed out to sea, at no time coming closer than sixteen miles to the coast of North Vietnam. At 2040, Captain Herrick notified the *Ticonderoga* that he had received indication of an attack that appeared "imminent." He added the task group was "proceeding so'east at best speed." The destroyers were then more than sixty miles southeast of Hon Me.

A minute later, the *Maddox*'s radar picked up surface contact forty-two miles to the northeast, in the area where the task group had intended to cruise during the night. This radar contact set in motion a string of events that would soon become one of the most controversial actions of the Vietnam War.

Several elements influenced the unfolding events: personnel fatigue, differing radar tunings on each destroyer, and freak weather conditions—particularly a phenomenon peculiar to the gulf waters known as the Tonkin Gulf "ghosts," or Tonkin Spook. The so-called Tonkin Spook apparently caused bogus blips on a radarscope. According to retired Commander R.L. Schreadley of the navy, false radar contacts in the Gulf of Tonkin were "widely noted but never adequately explained."

As commander of the USS *Blakely*, a destroyer escort operating in the gulf in 1973, Schreadley witnessed the phenomenon himself on his surface-search radar. A formation of rapidly closing contacts appeared on screen, so realistic that his weapons officer wanted to fire on them. Schreadley later recalled the experience:

> I hesitated. The contacts were speeding across the radar scope faster than any surface contact I had ever seen. Could they be low-flying aircraft? If so, whose? Even as I watched, the contacts sharp and well-defined one moment, vanished the next. From conversations I later had with other ship captains, I am convinced that the *Blakely*'s experience was far from

unique. The Tonkin Gulf ghosts most often were attributed to freak weather conditions or "ducting" of electromagnetic waves.

Radar waves generally travel in straight lines. Ducting occurs when atmospheric conditions force radar waves to follow the earth's curvature. It may take place in very calm weather, for example, when a blanket of warm moist air sits just above the surface of the sea and is not scattered by wind. Such conditions did not exist on the night of August 4, however.

Weather conditions in the Gulf of Tonkin that night included a ten- to twenty-knot wind from the southeast and intermittent thunderstorms and rain squalls. Cloud cover lay at about two thousand feet, over a moderate sea with two- to six-foot waves. The night was moonless and dark. Under such conditions, targets can be tracked intermittently by radar out to very long distances. As Captain Bryce D. Inman, an expert on radar, has observed, "With a number of 'intermittent' returns it is possible to construct a radar track that goes almost anywhere at any speed you want to imagine." In other words, intermittent returns are unreliable.

Differences in radar tuning added to the confusion. The *Maddox*, in the lead position, was responsible for long-range radar observation of potential enemies. Holding station some one thousand yards astern of the *Maddox*, the *C. Turner Joy* was charged with ensuring the two vessels did not collide during tactical maneuvering or evasive actions. Accordingly, its radar was tuned for short-range operation.

Operating at high power, the radar could detect targets at long range but at a cost of increased "surface clutter," that is, radar reflections off wave tops. Such reflections tended to mask closer targets. Reduced power rendered sharper images of nearby targets on the radar screen but made it difficult to pick up targets at long ranges. Moreover, the differences in their radar tunings prevented the ships from comparing and confirming similar radar contacts. Many radar experts now believe it likely that low-flying American aircraft caused some of the radar contacts that night.

Another, no less critical factor, was the increased stress caused by having been attacked two days earlier. Long hours at general quarters prolonged the tension after the first incident, and the personnel on both destroyers were fatigued. Stress and weariness rarely make for clear thinking. Such were the conditions facing the officers and enlisted men of the *Maddox* and the *C. Turner Joy* on the night of August 4, 1964.

At 2107, *Maddox* radar operators determined that three Swatows and P-4s detected earlier had joined in close formation and drawn within thirty-two miles of the two destroyers. Herrick ordered a bearing change to the southeast and the two ships began a dash toward the carrier task group at a speed of thirty knots. Not quite a half-hour later, an F-8E, piloted by Commander James B. Stockdale, and two A-4D Skyhawks from the *Ticonderoga* arrived to fly air cover over the two ships. Before the night ended, another thirteen aircraft from the *Ticonderoga* and the *Constellation* would be scrambled and sent to fly combat air patrols overhead.

At 2215, both destroyers detected three or four radar contacts in close formation about thirteen miles astern that were closing in fast. Fire-control radar on both ships tracked these targets as they approached to within 23,200 yards. Suddenly, both vessels detected still another contact only ninety-eight hundred yards due east, coming on fast at thirty-five to forty knots. When the latter target drew within seven thousand yards, the *C. Turner Joy* opened fire. The *Maddox* quickly followed suit. Almost simultaneously, the craft turned left and sped off.

Lieutenant Frederick Frick, the watch officer in the *Maddox*'s combat information center, plotted and recorded the maneuver on his dead-reckoning tracer and evaluated it as a torpedo launch. At the same time, a *Maddox* sonarman reported hearing torpedo noises. Commander Ogier immediately ordered the *Maddox* to come full right rudder to parallel the track of the torpedo. He warned the *C. Turner Joy*, which came hard right on course.

Lieutenant John Barry, the officer in charge of Fire Control Director 51 on the *C. Turner Joy*, the ship's main gun director located high in the superstructure, spied "a distinct wake on port side about 5 hundred feet from the ship moving from forward on a parallel course to this ship . . . The wake itself appeared light in color and more just below the surface than anything cutting the water on the surface and . . . it performed a definite vee in the water." Three other crewmen aboard the destroyer also reported having sighted the torpedo wake some one hundred to five hundred feet to port.

Numerous other radar contacts, sightings of torpedoes in the water, and rapid-fire responses at fast-moving targets occurred over the next two hours. The two destroyers began steaming independently, firing reactively at targets that suddenly appeared on radarscopes and quickly disappeared. Three sailors aboard the *C. Turner Joy*—Boatswain's Mate Third Class Donald Sharkey, Seaman Kenneth Garrison, and Gunner's Mate Delner Jones—saw what they said was a torpedo boat silhouetted briefly in the light of a star shell. "[The] outline of this contact was clearly seen by me and was definitely a PT boat," said Sharkey.

Garrison concurred, adding, "I saw it long enough to make sure what it was." A few sailors reported seeing a bright light—possibly a searchlight aimed skyward—aft of the *C. Turner Joy*. Others observed machine-gun fire raking the water close to the ship. Convinced that torpedo boats were following in their wake, both the *Maddox* and the *C. Turner Joy* dropped depth charges.

Shortly after 2300, radarmen on the *C. Turner Joy* picked up several contacts between two thousand and six thousand yards to the west. The ship fired briefly on the fleeting targets, plotting one target dead in the water and presuming it sunk. Verification was not possible. Soon afterward, about 2328, a second contact drew within twenty-five hundred yards and the destroyer's guns pounded away at it. Crewmen saw several explosions and radarmen witnessed many hits on the target. Commander Robert Barnhardt, captain of the *C. Turner Joy*, along with a few others, saw a thick column of black smoke rise from the target area. They presumed the boat sunk.

Meanwhile, overhead, most of the pilots of the sixteen aircraft did not see any enemy surface craft. Commander Stockdale, in particular, declared then and throughout the years afterward that he had seen nothing during an hour and thirty-five minutes on the scene. During a 1996 interview, Stockdale, then a retired admiral and holder of the Medal of Honor, said:

> Never saw anything but the two destroyers and their gun fire. And occasionally the airplanes that I knew where they were . . . And these ADs [A-4D Skyhawks] got out there about the time they opened gun fire. And they were down and they would have lights on and I could see them, but there was nothing in the water. There were no wakes.

Despite Stockdale's insistence that there were no enemy surface craft present that night, two of his fellow pilots added conflicting information to the mix. Commander George Edmondson and his wingman Lieutenant Jere A. Barton, both piloting slow-flying A-1H Skyraiders off the *Ticonderoga*, claimed to have seen what they took for antiaircraft fire. An hour later, Edmondson saw a "snakey" high-speed phosphorescent wake in the water about a mile and a half ahead of the *Maddox*, the lead ship. And on another pass, Barton spotted a "dark object" in the wake between the two destroyers that soon moved away from the ships and out of sight.

Of an early morning debriefing on August 5, Edmondson says, "The debrief was very short. As I recall the only question asked was did we see any enemy PT boats? The answer was no." He later acknowledged he "had seen surface gunfire" but at a distance that he "took to be from our destroyers." Edmondson also came to believe—but not until a long time later—that the snake-like wake had "most probably" been created by wave action. Barton died in 1970, having said very little about his experiences that night.

The last of the radar contacts disappeared from the scopes of both destroyers just before 0100 on August 5, 1964, and the *Maddox* and the *C. Turner Joy* resumed their run toward the carrier task group. During some four hours of bizarre action, the two warships had fired 249 five-inch shells—including twenty-four star shells—and 123 three-inch rounds. They also dropped four or five depth charges against boats believed to have been trailing in their wakes.

Many—if not most—of the personnel of the *Maddox* and the *C. Turner Joy* came away from the incident convinced they had experienced a real attack by a real enemy. Yet, over the years, many military analysts and students of the phenomenon have come to believe the only contacts present during the entire second incident were the Tonkin Gulf ghosts.

Chapter Ten

Retaliation and Escalation

During the frenzied atmosphere of the second incident in two days in the Gulf of Tonkin, Captain John J. Herrick counted a total of twenty-two enemy torpedoes, none of which had scored a hit. He also reported sinking two and maybe three Communist vessels during the frantic four-hour sea battle. However, in the immediate aftermath of the "spooky" engagement, Herrick started experiencing second thoughts about the fray. He communicated his doubts to Pacific Fleet commander Admiral Moorer aboard the *Ticonderoga*: "Freak weather effects on radar and overeager sonarmen may have accounted for many reports. No actual visual sightings by *Maddox*. Suggest complete evaluation before any further action taken."

Herrick had earlier claimed the North Vietnamese set up an ambush for the two destroyers. He never retracted his original contention, stating only that he could not confirm the torpedoes. In another report, he suggested some of the radar contacts might have been enemy PT boats feinting at the destroyers.

About the same time, in an early debriefing aboard the *Ticonderoga* on August 5, 1964, an intelligence officer asked James Stockdale if he had seen any enemy boats. Commander Stockdale, who had enjoyed "the best seat in the house from which to detect boats," as he later put it, answered, "No boats, no boat wakes, no ricochets off boats, no boat impacts, no torpedo wakes—nothing but the black sea and American firepower."

Admiral Moorer sent Herrick's message and Stockdale's statements to Admiral Sharp in Hawaii, who in turn flashed it to the Joint Chiefs of Staff in Washington. Neither the Joint Chiefs nor the Johnson administration was happy to see the after-battle musings. The Joint Chiefs fired back a message to Admiral Sharp, urgently requesting "evidence of second attack [to] convince United Nations that the attack did in fact occur." The Joint Chiefs were working frantically to draft plans for a retaliatory strike against North Vietnam.

Meanwhile, although not a single correspondent had been present during either incident in the gulf, the news media was already publishing dramatized accounts of the second event, embellished with the help of the Pentagon. "The night glowed eerily," noted *Time*, as Communist "intruders boldly sped" toward the American destroyers, blazing away with "automatic weapons." *Life* magazine, which was owned by the same company that published *Time*, portrayed the two ships "under continuous torpedo attack" as they "weaved through the night sea, evading more torpedoes."

Not to be outdone, *Newsweek* depicted "U.S. jets diving, strafing, flattening out . . . and diving again" at the attacking boats, one of which "burst into flames and sank." The attack on U.S. naval vessels led *Newsweek* to conclude, "It was time for American might to strike back."

Anti-Communist sentiment and anger swelled once again in Washington, D.C. Several Democratic congressmen cautioned President Johnson that he was "being tested." He would have to respond firmly to the North Vietnamese provocation, they said, or leave himself open to attack by presidential rival Barry Goldwater and the Republican right wing, which was stridently pro-war. Johnson pressured Secretary of Defense McNamara to confirm if the second attack had taken place.

The secretary telephoned Sharp on a secure line and queried him about the latest information. He wanted strong confirmation the second attack did occur, but the admiral was not ready to commit himself. "How do we reconcile all this?" McNamara asked. Sharp told him to wait a couple of hours for more information. While McNamara waited impatiently, Admiral Sharp conferred with Admiral Moorer and tried to piece together all reports.

"After a few hours, Admiral Moorer and I decided that there was enough information available to indicate that an attack had, in fact, occurred," Sharp wrote later. "Accordingly, I called McNamara and informed him of our evaluation, indicating that, while reports from the ships were not conclusive by themselves, the weight of evidence (including some radio intercept intelligence) supported our conclusion."

McNamara informed the president of the admirals' conclusions. Despite the lack of hard evidence, Johnson ordered retaliatory strikes against North Vietnam to commence that evening. He left it to the secretary to justify his action to Congress.

For McNamara, the radio intercepts carried most of the burden of proof, and he used them as his principal points in a Congressional hearing to show evidence of the second attack. A few days later, however, a CIA analyst carefully examined the radio intercepts and concluded they actually related to the first attack.

In Washington, D.C., in the early evening of August 4, the president met with sixteen key congressional leaders. Acting on the sketchy information available to him, he informed them the two U.S. warships in the Tonkin Gulf had definitely been attacked, and he had ordered retaliatory air strikes. Johnson also called on Dean Rusk, McNamara, CIA Director John McCone, and Joint Chiefs of Staff Chairman General Earle Wheeler to brief the representatives. Each of these men emphasized the unprovoked nature of the attacks and the urgent need for a display of American resolve.

The meeting succeeded in winning senate support. Only Senate Majority Leader Mike Mansfield opposed retaliation. "The Communists won't be forced down," he said, adding that any effort in that regard would only cost "a lot of lives." Mansfield, who had initially been a supporter of Johnson's policies in Vietnam, was starting to believe a military solution was not possible. He thought the problems in Vietnam required diplomacy. Mansfield, however, was in the clear minority.

Johnson turned to the subject of a congressional resolution, which he had already discussed with several of the legislators earlier that day. The formal resolution granting the president extraordinary war powers had been drafted months earlier. It had been shelved until after the upcoming election—or until the occurrence of a dramatic turn of events in Southeast Asia. It had been decided that the dramatic event had occurred, although there was still no solid confirmation the second attack had taken place.

"I have told you what I want from you," Johnson said, before going around the room asking each legislator how he stood on passage of the resolution. Everyone, including Mansfield, offered his support.

George Aiken, Republican senator from Vermont, summed up the general mood of his colleagues. "By the time you send [the resolution] up here there won't be anything for us to [do] but support you," he told Johnson. It would be political suicide to refuse to support the president, and the troops, when American ships had come under attack.

President Johnson had the congressional support he wanted. After the meeting, he received a call from Republican presidential nominee Senator Barry Goldwater, who offered his support for retaliatory air strikes.

At 11:36 P.M., President Johnson faced the television cameras and told the nation of the air strikes that he had ordered against North Vietnam. As he spoke, the first planes had left the *Ticonderoga*, but additional aircraft had yet to leave the *Constellation*. He concluded his six-minute address, saying, "We seek no wider war."

Hanoi did not believe the president, who during his address had not told the American people about the U.S.-directed covert activities that had been conducted against North Vietnam over the past months. Hanoi did not believe the American denials of any link between covert marops and the DeSoto patrols.

Hanoi's perception of the marops-DeSoto connection became clear when the North Vietnamese Ministry of Foreign Affairs later issued a "Memorandum Regarding the U.S. War Acts Against the Democratic Republic of Vietnam in the First Days of August 1964." The memo pointed out actions that Washington denied:

> On July 30, 1964 . . . U.S. and South Vietnamese warships intruded into the territorial waters of the Democratic Republic of Vietnam and simultaneously shelled: Hon Nieu [Ngu] Island, 4 kilometers [2.5 miles] off the coast of Thanh Hoa Province [and] Hon Me Island, 12 kilometers [7.5 miles] off the coast of Thanh Hoa Province.

The memorandum also depicted the *Maddox*'s path

along the North Vietnamese coast on August 2, and described the 34A attacks on Vinh Son the next day. Hanoi also flatly denied American claims it had fired on the U.S. destroyers on August 4 in the Gulf of Tonkin, calling the charge an "impudent fabrication."

Few would deny North Vietnam had some justification for bristling at U.S. naval presence in the Gulf of Tonkin, or in distrusting Washington's reports about what happened there. As Edwin E. Moïse, a leading authority on the Tonkin Gulf affair, points out, "Had the Soviet Union put such a vessel [one equipped with five-inch guns] off Charleston during a week when the Soviet Union was also sending Cuban gunboats to shell the South Carolina coast, it is unlikely that it could have remained there even twenty-four hours without being attacked by U.S. forces."

Regardless of Hanoi's denials, Johnson and his advisors viewed the Tonkin Gulf incidents as the opportunity they had been waiting for. Now that the flag had been fired upon, Johnson could escalate the war in Vietnam. He and his advisors thought that once the might of the United States entered the conflict, tiny North Vietnam would soon sue for a negotiated settlement. The American leaders thought it was the best solution to a difficult problem. Of course, taking action would also silence Johnson's right-wing critics—which would kill Goldwater's already slim chances of winning the November election. The president expected only a handful of lawmakers would stand in his way.

To insure speedy passage of the Tonkin Gulf Resolution, Johnson enlisted the aid of Democratic Senator William J. Fulbright of Arkansas, an old friend and colleague from his days in Congress, to shepherd it through the Senate. Although Fulbright, head of the Senate Foreign Relations Committee, had reservations about the war in Vietnam and recognized the dangers inherent in the wording of the resolution, which gave the president almost unlimited authority, he knew he could not oppose the president on an issue of patriotism. He agreed to manage the resolution to certain passage. This was a decision he would regret later, when he turned against the war.

On August 5, the day after the reported second attack, President Johnson sent his resolution requesting war powers in Vietnam to Congress. Senator Wayne Morse, once a Republican but now a Democrat from Oregon, immediately called on Fulbright to hold full-fledged Senate hearings on the resolution. Morse cautioned him that the wording of the measure was far too general and open-ended to entrust to any president. Fulbright answered that the urgency of the situation did not allow time to hold formal Senate hearings.

The next day, Secretary of Defense McNamara appeared before a joint session of the Senate Foreign Relations and Armed Services Committees. He told the senators the North Vietnamese attack on the *Maddox* was "no isolated event. They are part and parcel of a continuing Communist drive to conquer South Vietnam." McNamara failed to mention the direct U.S. involvement in the covert 34A operations.

A skeptical Wayne Morse, tipped off by a Pentagon staffer, pressed McNamara on the link between the 34A ops and the DeSoto patrols. Journalist David Halberstam has described Morse as "irascible, forceful, an expert on international law and Lyndon Johnson" and "as a man willing to go it alone on an issue of conscience." Despite evidence to the contrary, the senator concluded, it seemed obvious the two missions were operating in tandem. "I think we are kidding the world," he scolded McNamara, "if you try to give the impression that when the South Vietnamese naval boats bombarded two islands a short distance off the coast of North Vietnam we were not implicated."

McNamara denied any connection between the two missions. The attacks, he said, were "deliberate and unprovoked" against U.S. warships on "routine patrol in international waters." The secretary went on to state emphatically, "Our navy played absolutely no part in, was not associated with, [and] was not aware of any South Vietnamese actions, if there were any." McNamara's critics insist his latter statement was an absolute lie. McNamara claimed he did not learn until later that Captain Herrick had had full knowledge of the 34A operations.

Senator Morse, because of the secrecy surrounding the covert operations, did not have enough information to ask more probing questions. He met with resistance when he tried to interest other senators in pursuing the connection further. One fellow lawmaker told him: "Hell, Wayne, you can't get in a fight with the President at a time when the flags are waving and we're about to go to a national convention. All Lyndon wants is a piece of paper telling him we did right out there, and we support him." Morse's colleague went on to assure him that Johnson was "the kind of president who follows the rules and won't get the country into war without coming back to Congress."

On August 7, 1964, Congress passed the Gulf of Tonkin Resolution authorizing President Lyndon Baines Johnson to use "all necessary measures" to repel armed attacks against U.S. forces in Vietnam. The resolution passed on a vote of eighty-eight to two in the Senate and a unanimous 416 to zero in the House of Representatives. Senators Wayne Morse and Ernest Gruening, a Democrat from Alaska and a long-standing critic of U.S. involvement in Vietnam, were the only dissenters. After the vote, Senator Morse told his colleagues:

> I believe that history will record that we have made a great mistake in subverting and circumventing the Constitution of the United States . . . by means of this resolution. As I argued earlier today at great length, we are in effect giving the President . . . war making powers in the absence of a declaration of war. I believe that to be a historic mistake.

In retrospect, Senator Morse could not have been more right. In theory, the Gulf of Tonkin Resolution was not the same as a declaration of war; in practice, however, it granted singular war-making powers to the

President Johnson visited soldiers stationed at Cam Ranh Bay in December 1967. *(AP Photo.)*

president and enabled him to conduct a long, bloody war without having to return to Congress for more support. Congress could have rescinded the resolution at any time, but it did not do so until more than six years later, in December, 1970. By then, tens of thousands of American and countless Vietnamese lives had been lost in a war the United States could not—and did not—win.

It seems clear to many critics today that, had the Johnson administration revealed all the circumstances surrounding the incidents in the gulf, Congress would have at least held hearings on the resolution before voting. Had Congress delved deeper into the facts, some members might have voted differently on the measure. It is still probable the resolution would have passed. The pressures of an election year and the ongoing Cold War against Communist expansion made it very difficult for any elected official to vote against supporting the military when it was viewed to be in harm's way. Hearings, at least, would have allowed for a clearer understanding of what actually happened in the international waters off the coast of Vietnam.

Some detractors of the Johnson administration and American involvement in Vietnam even suggest the president and his advisors deliberately staged the events in the gulf to provoke a North Vietnamese response in order to facilitate the passage of the resolution. When questioned about this later, during an interview on British radio, George Ball, former U.S. undersecretary of state, answered:

> Many of the people who were associated with the war . . . were looking for any excuse to initiate bombing . . . The Desoto patrol was primarily for provocation . . . There was a feeling that if the destroyer got into some trouble, that would provide the provocation we needed.

Conversely, in addressing the same question later, former Undersecretary of State William Bundy, a chief drafter of the Gulf of Tonkin Resolution and a pro-bombing advocate, wrote the evidence supporting the

President Johnson consulted former President and General Dwight Eisenhower about the Vietnam War. *(Courtesy of the Lyndon Baines Johnson Library. Photo by Yokimo R. Okamoto.)*

idea that the administration provoked "the incidents is not simply weak, it is nonexistent." He credited the cause of the incidents to a miscalculation on the part of both the U.S. and North Vietnam:

> In simple terms, it was a mistake for an Administration sincerely resolved to keep its risks low, to have the 34A operations and the destroyer patrol take place even in the same time period. Rational minds could not readily have foreseen that Hanoi might confuse them . . . but rational calculations should have taken account of the irrational . . . Washington did not want an incident, and it seems doubtful that

Hanoi did either. Yet each misread the other, and the incidents happened.

Although these opinions seem to conflict, former Secretary of Defense Robert McNamara wrote in his memoirs he agreed with both points of view. He stated, "The idea that the Johnson administration deliberately deceived Congress is false." Rather, he writes, "The problem was not that Congress did not grasp the resolution's potential but that it did not grasp the war's potential and how the administration would respond in the face of it." When he appeared before Congress, McNamara had full knowledge of the 34A operations against the North Vietnamese islands of Hon Me and Hon Ngu.

Three months after the passage of the Gulf of Tonkin Resolution, Lyndon Johnson, the "peace candidate," defeated Barry Goldwater, the "war hawk," in a land-slide election. In March 1965, U.S. aircraft began bombing North Vietnam and U.S. ground troops landed *en masse* in South Vietnam. America had openly entered into the war in Vietnam.

Afterword

On February 27, 1968, Walter Cronkite, at the time probably America's most respected television newscaster, returned from a visit to Vietnam and gloomily reported it appeared "more certain than ever that the bloody experience of Vietnam is to end in a stalemate." Since Cronkite's earlier reporting on the war had been balanced and noncommittal, this prediction shocked the nation. Cronkite's report, combined with the disappointing progress in the Vietnam War, disheartened President Johnson.

On March 31, 1968, Johnson went on prime-time television to announce plans to deescalate the war. He ended his address with a statement that surprised the nation: He had decided not to run for reelection. After Republican Richard Nixon defeated Johnson's vice president, Hubert Humphrey, in one of the closest elections ever, Johnson returned home to his Texas ranch in 1969. That same year, America's commitment to the ultimately

Despite his efforts, President Johnson was not able to stop the Communist North Vietnamese. *(Courtesy of the Lyndon Baines Johnson Library. Photo by Yoichi R. Okamoto.)*

unsuccessful war in Vietnam peaked with 550,000 military personnel in the country. Johnson died on January 22, 1973, five days before the Paris Agreement to end the war and restore peace in Vietnam was signed.

Robert McNamara left office in February 1968, amid a raging debate over U.S. Vietnam policy. His detractors have pointed out his emphasis on sophisticated management techniques and his belief that a war should be run like a corporation led to many misperceptions about the realities of the war in Vietnam.

General William C. Westmoreland, who took the heat for many of the failures in Vietnam, returned to Washington in July 1968 and served as chairman of the Joint Chiefs of Staff until his retirement in 1972.

On April 8, 1987, James B. Stockdale, by then a retired admiral and recipient of the Medal of Honor, addressed the American Society of Newspaper Editors in San Francisco. He described himself as "the only person in the world who was an eyewitness to both the actions of the real PT boats on Sunday [August 2, 1964] and the 'phantom battle' on Tuesday night [August 4, 1964]." Stockdale stated his belief that America's "best and brightest" had deceived the nation.

"What the hell kind of scale of values has this twen-

Millions of people visit the Vietnam Veteran's Memorial in Washington, D.C., each year. The Wall, as it has come to be called, is inscribed with the names of the 58,229 American men and women who died in the war. *(Courtesy of the Library of Congress.)*

tieth century world lured us into?" he asked. He went on:

> Those Whiz Kids [of the Johnson Administration] and their mentors played games with the great good will of Middle America, squandered it, 'got religion,' bugged out, left a generation of their sons face down in the mud, and got away with it. They bragged about running a war without emotional involvement of the mob, the men on the street. They decided it was best to keep the American public in the dark, and rely on their own 'creative thinking.'

One of the great ironies of the Tonkin Gulf affair, and of the legacy it leaves for America, can be found in the memoirs of Robert McNamara. He asks the question "should a president take our nation to war (other than immediately to repel an attack on our shores) without popular consent as voiced by Congress?" How much power to make war should be handed over to the few, mainly non-elected, figures who advise the president, and how much should be confined to the much wider body of representatives that the American people have elected and sent to Washington, D.C.? This question was crucial in the twentieth century, and is perhaps even more crucial today.

Appendix

The Gulf of Tonkin Resolution

Joint Resolution of Congress H.J. Res 1145 August 7, 1964

Resolved by the Senate and House of Representatives of the United States of America in Congress assembled,

That the Congress approves and supports the determination of the President, as Commander in Chief, to take all necessary measures to repel any armed attack against the forces of the United States and to prevent further aggression.

Section 2. The United States regards as vital to its national interests and to world peace the maintenance of international peace and security in Southeast Asia. Consonant with the Constitution of the United States and the Charter of the United Nations and in accordance with its obligations under the Southeast Asia Collective Defense Treaty, the United States is, therefore, prepared, as the President determines, to take all necessary steps, including the use of armed force, to assist any member or protocol state of the Southeast Asia Collective Defense Treaty requesting assistance in defense of its freedom.

Section 3. This resolution shall expire when the President shall determine that the peace and security of the area is reasonably assured by international conditions created by the United Nations or otherwise, except that it may be terminated earlier by concurrent resolution of the Congress.

(Source: Department of State Bulletin, August 24, 1964.)

Glossary

ARVN: Army of the Republic of (South) Vietnam.

bathythermograph: A device for measuring water temperature and depth.

Biet Hai: Literally, "sea commandos" of the SouthVietnamese Navy.

CIA: Central Intelligence Agency of the United States.

comvan: Communications van; a shipping van loaded with radio equipment for electronic intelligence gathering.

coup: A brilliant, sudden, and usually successful stroke or act; coup d'état (stroke of state), the violent overthrow or alteration of an existing government by a small group.

dau tranh: Vietnamese for "struggle."

dau tranh chinh tri: Vietnamese for "political struggle."

dau tranh vu trang: Vietnamese for "armed struggle."

DeSoto: Code name for electronic reconnaissance patrols conducted by specially equipped U.S. naval vessels in the Gulf of Tonkin and elsewhere.

DRV: Democratic Republic of (North) Vietnam, seated in Hanoi.

ECM: Electronic Counter Measures.

Gulf of Tonkin Resolution: A Congressional resolution (officially the Southeast Asia Resolution) empowering the president "to take all necessary measures to repel any armed attack against the forces of the United States and to prevent further aggression." On August 7, 1964, it passed the Senate by a vote of 88 to 2 and the House by a unanimous vote of 416 to 0. Congress repealed the resolution in May 1970.

Ho Chi Minh Trail: A network of roads stretching from North Vietnam through Laos into South Vietnam; the main supply route for troops and material in support of Hanoi's war against the Saigon government.

knot: A nautical mile (1.15 statute miles); one nautical mile per hour.

***Lien Doi Nguoi Nhai,* or LDNN:** Literally, "frogman unit;" South Vietnamese special operations unit.

logistics: The organization of supplies and services, etc.

MACV: Military Assistance Command Vietnam.

marops: Covert maritime (or marine) operations.

NSAM 288: National Security Action Memorandum redefining and expanding U.S. objectives in South Vietnam and Southeast Asia.

Nasty: High-speed, heavily armed, Norwegian-built patrol boat (PTF).

OPLAN 34A: Operations Plan 34A; a U.S. plan for covert operations against North Vietnam, carried out by South Vietnamese personnel inserted north of the 17th parallel by air, sea, and land.

PCF: Patrol Craft, Fast.

P-4: Soviet-built torpedo boat.

PTF: Patrol Type (or Torpedo), Fast.

RVN: Republic of (South) Vietnam, seated in Saigon.

SEAL: Special warfare unit of the United States Navy, named for the first letters of the elements by which they infiltrate, operate, and disengage—*SE*a-*A*ir-*L*and.

SEATO: Southeast Asia Treaty Organization; an organization founded in 1954 to bind together the non-Communist nations of the region as a curb to Communist expansion.

seventeenth parallel: Line established by the Geneva Accords to separate North and South Vietnam until free elections could be held.

SOG: Special Operations Group, responsible for U.S. military covert operations in Vietnam and Laos; later assigned the less-revealing name of Studies and Observation Group; also MACVSOG or MACSOG.

starboard quarter: Right-hand stern side of a ship.

star shell: A shell with an illuminating projectile.

surface clutter: Radar reflections off wave tops.

Swatow: Chinese-built gunboat.

Swift: Fast, heavily armed, American-built patrol boat (PCF).

teleprinter: A device that produces hard copy from signals received over a communications circuit.

transceiver: A combined radio receiver and transmitter.

Vietcong: A contraction of *Viet Nam Cong San*, or Vietnamese Communist; guerrilla forces in South Vietnam comprising a core of former members of the Vietminh who had remained in southern Vietnam, plus new members recruited from the southern population.

Vietminh: A contraction of *Vietnam Doc Lap Dong Minh*, or League for Vietnamese Independence; Vietnamese forces—both Communist and Nationalist—who fought the French from 1946 to 1954.

Zuni: A large supersonic rocket, five feet in diameter and more than nine feet long, weighing 107 pounds.

Timeline

1964 Tonkin Gulf Affair

July 30-31—South Vietnamese commandos operating out of Da Nang—under SOG direction—conduct raids against North Vietnamese offshore islands of Hon Me and Hon Ngu.

August 2— U.S. destroyer *Maddox* attacked by three North Vietnamese torpedo boats while on an intelligence-gathering reconnaissance DeSoto patrol in the Gulf of Tonkin.

August 3— U.S. destroyer *Maddox*, joined by the U.S. destroyer *C. Turner Joy*, reenters the Gulf of Tonkin.

August 4— The *Maddox* and the *C. Turner Joy* report being attacked by North Vietnamese vessels southeast of Hon Me; President Lyndon B. Johnson announces a second attack on American war ships and authorizes a retaliatory air strike— Operation Pierce Arrow—on North Vietnamese bases.

August 5— Operation Pierce Arrow carried out; President Johnson sends war-powers resolution (prepared and refined several months earlier) to Congress.

August 6— Secretary of Defense Robert S. McNamara testifies before Congress about the Tonkin Gulf incidents.

August 7— Congress passes the Gulf of Tonkin Resolution.

November 3—President Johnson defeats rival Barry Goldwater in a landslide presidential election.

Sources

CHAPTER ONE: Containing Communism

p. 11, "fellow Americans" Ezra Y. Siff, *Why the Senate Slept: The Gulf of Tonkin Resolution and the Beginning of America's Vietnam War.* (Westport, CT: Praeger, 1999), 113

p. 11, "As President and Commander in Chief . . ." Ibid.

p. 12, "now in execution . . ." Ibid.

p. 12, "new act of aggression," Ibid., 114.

p. 12, "that our Government is united . . ." Ibid.

p. 12, "that firmness in the right . . ." Ibid.

p. 13, "Its mission is peace," Ibid.

CHAPTER TWO: Defeat of the French

p. 21, "long-term, patient but firm and vigilant . . ." Robert Mann, *A Grand Delusion: America's Descent into Vietnam* (New York: Basic Books, 2001), 23-24.

p. 21, "it must be the policy of the United States . . ." Thomas Parrish, *The Cold War Encyclopedia* (New York: Henry Holt, 1996), 317.

p. 23, "loss of China" Ibid., 63.

CHAPTER THREE: Johnson Takes Charge

p. 25, "possibly 80 percent of the population . . ." Paul M. Taillon, "Elections, South Vietnam, 1955," in *Encyclopedia of the Vietnam War* (Edited by Stanley I. Kutler. New York: Simon & Schuster Macmillan, 1996), 190.

p. 25, "has not itself been party to . . ." Ronald E. Powaski, *The Cold War: The United States and the Soviet Union, 1917-1991* (New York: Oxford University Press, 1998), 109.

p. 26, "You have a row of dominoes . . ." Parrish, *The Cold War Encyclopedia*, 85-86.

p. 28, "The United States will . . ." Leo B. Ribuffo, "Eisenhower, Dwight D.," in *Encyclopedia of the Vietnam War* (Kutler), 189.

p. 28, "the cornerstone of the Free World . . ." Robert J. McMahon, "Kennedy, John F. (1917-1963)," in *Encyclopedia of the Vietnam War* (Kutler), 259.

p. 28, "a test of American responsibility . . ." Ibid.

p. 30, "anywhere, at anytime . . ." Powaski, *The Cold War*, 141.

p. 37, "urgently examine all possible alternate leadership . . ." Claude R. Sasso, "Kennedy, John Fitzgerald (1917-1963)," in *Encyclopedia of the Vietnam War: A Political, Social, and Military History* (Edited by Spencer C. Tucker. New York: Oxford University Press, 1998), 202.

CHAPTER FOUR: Covert Maritime Operations

p. 40, "Covert operations by . . ." Edwin E. Moïse, *Tonkin Gulf and the Escalation of the Vietnam War* (Chapel Hill, NC: University of North Carolina Press, 1996), 5.

p. 42, "small unspectacular raids" Kenneth Conboy and Dale Andradé, *Spies and Commandos: How America Lost the Secret War in North Vietnam* (Lawrence, KS: University Press of Kansas, 2000), 92.

p. 42, "aerial attacks conducted . . ." Moïse, *Tonkin Gulf and the Escalation of the Vietnam War*, 5.

p. 42, "in concert with . . ." Ibid.

p. 42, "to escalate the conflict . . ." Ibid.

p. 44, "to respond to the exigencies . . ." Glen Gendzel, "Nguyen Khanh," in *Encyclopedia of the Vietnam War* (Kutler), 362.

p. 44, "fight communism . . ." Ibid.

p. 46, "harassment and short-term sabotage raids . . ." Richard H. Schultz, Jr., *The Secret War Against Hanoi: Kennedy's and Johnson's Use of Spies, Saboteurs, and Covert Warriors in North Vietnam* (New York: Harper Collins Publishers, 1999), 163-64.

p. 46, "proposed the use of . . ." Ibid., 164.

p. 47, "a step in the right . . ." Ibid.

p. 47, "priority attention also be given . . ." Ibid.

p. 47, "take immediate action . . ." Ibid.

p. 48, "make it clear . . ." John L. Plaster, *SOG: The Secret Wars of America's Commandos in Vietnam* (New York: Penguin Putnam, 1998), 23.

p. 48, "those that provide . . ." Ibid.

p. 50, "Five attempts to infiltrate . . ." Moïse, *Tonkin Gulf and the Escalation of the Vietnam War*, 16.

CHAPTER FIVE: Planning Ahead

p. 52, "I am not going to lose . . ." Powaski, *The Cold War*, 155.

p. 52, "it might as well . . ." Ibid.

p. 52, "durability, resolution . . ." Stanley Karnow, *Vietnam: A History*. Rev. ed. (New York: Viking, 1991), 342.

p. 52, "our image" Ibid.

p. 52, "increasingly bolder" Ibid.

p. 53, "the actual direction . . ." Ibid.

p. 53, "soft on Communism" Ibid.

p. 53, "Just get me elected . . ." Ibid.

p. 54, "Contingency planning for . . ." Moïse, *Tonkin Gulf and the Escalation of the Vietnam War*, 22-23.

p. 54, "DeSoto differed substantially . . ." Robert S. McNamara, with Brian VanDeMark, *In Retrospect: The Tragedy and Lessons of Vietnam* (New York: Times Books, 1995), 130.

p. 54, "They were part of . . ." Ibid.

p. 56, "Long before the August events . . ." Ibid.

p. 56, "the South Vietnamese saw them . . ." Ibid.

p. 57, "The situation has unquestionably . . ." Phillip B. Davidson, *Vietnam at War: The History: 1946-1975* (New York: Oxford University Press, 1991), 314.

p. 57, "1. In terms of government control . . ." Ibid.

p. 57, "win their contest . . ." Ibid.

p. 58, "We seek an independent . . ." Ibid.

p. 58, "Unless we can achieve . . ." Ibid., 314-15.

p. 59, "The broadened objectives . . ." Ibid., 315.

p. 60, "to make military action . . ." Moïse, *Tonkin Gulf and the Escalation of the Vietnam War*, 26.

p. 60, "wider action" Robert Mann, *A Grand Delusion: America's Descent into Vietnam* (New York: Basic Books, 2001), 333.

p. 61, "The United States regards . . ." Ibid.

p. 61, "To this end, if the President . . ." Ibid.

p. 61, "war fever" Ibid.

p. 61, "in the event of a dramatic event . . ." Moïse, *Tonkin Gulf and the Escalation of the Vietnam War*, 30.

CHAPTER SIX: Troubled Waters

p. 65, "might be good training . . ." Conboy and Andradé, *Spies and Commandos*, 108.

p. 65, "lack of adequate intelligence . . ." Ibid.

p. 65, "increased state of alert . . ." Ibid.

p. 65, "The odds against . . ." Ibid.

p. 65, "I have been watching . . ." Ibid.

p. 66, "more extensive and effective . . ." Ibid.

p. 66, "While we are wholly in favor . . ." Ibid.

p. 66, "This program will not . . ." Ibid.

p. 66, "embodied destruction of greater scope . . ." Schultz, *The Secret War Against Hanoi*, 177.

p. 68, "I would note that . . ." Ibid.

CHAPTER SEVEN: The First Sign of Trouble

p. 72, "had been built on a shoestring . . ." Moïse, *Tonkin Gulf and the Escalation of the Vietnam War*, 53.

p. 72, "was standard radio equipment . . ." Ibid.

p. 73, "leisure cruise" Ibid., 55.

p. 73, "a significant event" Ibid., 56.

p. 75, "The whole port bow . . ." Conboy and Andradé, *Spies and Commandos*, 117.

p. 75, "We were sad . . ." Ibid., 118.

p. 76, "well executed and highly successful . . ." Plaster, *SOG*, 27.

p. 76, "discussed in detail" Moïse, *Tonkin Gulf and the Escalation of the Vietnam War*, 59.

p. 76, "if 'quick reaction' tie-in . . ." Ibid.

p. 78, "Do not permit the guns . . ." Ibid., 62.

CHAPTER EIGHT: The First Incident: The *Real* Encounter

p. 80, "It came from a higher authority . . ." Moïse, *Tonkin Gulf and the Escalation of the Vietnam War*, 69.

p. 81, "If info received . . ." Ibid.

p. 81, "Approx 75 junks . . ." Moïse, *Tonkin Gulf and the Escalation of the Vietnam War*, 72.

p. 81, "No further evidence . . ." *Gulf of Tonkin Notebook*, (http://members.aol.com/warlibrary/vwton.htm), 3.

p. 82, "The PT boats were behind us . . ." Moïse, *Tonkin Gulf and the Escalation of the Vietnam War*, 75.

p. 83, "being approached by high-speed craft . . ." Conboy and Andradé, *Spies and Commandos*, 119.

p. 83, "to accomplish recon and weather missions . . ." Moïse, *Tonkin Gulf and the Escalation of the Vietnam War*, 62.

p. 85, "Because her torpedo was launched . . ." *Gulf of Tonkin Notebook*, (http://members.aol.com/warlibrary/vwton.htm), 4.

p. 86, "attacking boats were aggressive . . ." Ibid., 5.

p. 87, "at best speed" Moïse, *Tonkin Gulf and the Escalation of the Vietnam War*, 82.

p. 87, "the Zunis did not hit . . ." Ibid., 83.

CHAPTER NINE: The Second Incident: Ghosts in the Gulf

p. 89, "The group believed . . ." McNamara, *In Retrospect*, 131.

p. 90, "indication that the U.S. flinches . . ." Ibid.

p. 90, "Do they want a war . . ." *Naval History Magazine*, (http://www.usni.org/navalhistory/Articles99/NHandrade.htm), 8.

p. 90, "The North Vietnamese are reacting . . ." Ibid.

p. 92, "It is apparent that DRV . . ." *Gulf of Tonkin Notebook*, (http://members.aol.com/warlibrary/vwton.htm), 7.

p. 93, "In view [of the] Maddox incident . . ." Ibid., 6.

p. 93, "DRV PTs have advantage . . ." Ibid., 7.

p. 94, "imminent" Moïse, *Tonkin Gulf and the Escalation of the Vietnam War*, 113.

p. 94, "proceeding so'east . . ." *Gulf of Tonkin Notebook*, (http://members.aol.com/warlibrary/vwton.htm), 11.

p. 95, "widely noted but . . ." R. L. Schreadley, *From the Rivers to the Sea: The U.S. Navy in Vietnam* (Annapolis, MD: Naval Institute Press, 1992), 68.

p. 95, "I hesitated. The contacts were speeding . . ." Ibid., 69.

p. 96, "With a number of 'intermittent' returns . . ." Moïse, *Tonkin Gulf and the Escalation of the Vietnam War*, 115.

p. 98, "a distinct wake on port side . . ." *Gulf of Tonkin Notebook*, (http://members.aol.com/warlibrary/vwton.htm), 13.

p. 99, "The outline of this contact . . ." Ibid., 15.

p. 99, "I saw it long enough . . ." Ibid.

p. 100, "Never saw anything but . . ." *The Cold War: Episode 11: Vietnam* (http://www.gwu.edu/~nsarchiv/coldwar/interviews/episode-11/stockdale1.html), 6.

p. 100, "snakey" *Gulf of Tonkin Notebook*, (http://members.aol.com/warlibrary/vwton.htm), 14.

p. 101, "dark object" Schreadley, *From the Rivers to the Sea*, 66.

p. 101, "The debrief was very . . ." Moïse, *Tonkin Gulf and the Escalation of the Vietnam War*, 186.

p. 101, "had seen surface gunfire" Ibid., 188.

p. 101, "took to be from our destroyers." Ibid.

p. 101, "most probably" Ibid., 190.

CHAPTER TEN: Retaliation and Escalation

p. 102, "Freak weather effects on radar . . ." Lloyd C. Gardner, *Pay Any Price: Lyndon Johnson and the Wars for Vietnam* (Chicago: Ivan R. Dee, 1995), 137.

p. 103, "the best seat in the house . . ." Young, *The Vietnam Wars 1945-1990*, 118.

p. 103, "No boats, no boat wakes, no ricochets . . ." Ibid.

p. 103, "evidence of second attack . . ." Karnow, *Vietnam*, 386.

p. 103, "The night glowed eerily . . ." Ibid., 386-87.

p. 104, "U.S. jets diving, strafing, flattening out . . ." Ibid., 387.

p. 104, "It was time . . ." Ibid.

p. 104, "being tested" Ibid.

p. 104, "How do we reconcile . . ." Gardner, *Pay Any Price*, 137.

p. 104, "After a few hours, Admiral Moorer . . ." Ibid.

p. 106, "The Communists won't be . . ." Fredrik Logevall, *Choosing War: The Lost Chance for Peace and the Escalation of War in Vietnam* (Berkeley, CA: University of California Press, 1999), 199.

p. 106, "a lot of lives" Ibid.

p. 106, "I have told you what I want . . ." Ibid.

p. 106, "By the time you send . . ." Ibid.

p. 107, "We seek no wider . . ." Ibid.

p. 107, "On July 30, 1964 . . . U.S. and South Vietnamese . . ."
Naval History Magazine, (http://www.usni.org/
navalhistory/Articles99/NHandrade.htm), 8.

p. 108, "impudent fabrication" Ibid.

p. 108, "Had the Soviet Union put . . ." Moïse, *Tonkin Gulf
and the Escalation of the Vietnam War*, 68.

p. 109, "no isolated event. They are . . ." *Naval History
Magazine*, (http://www.usni.org/navalhistory/Articles99/
NHandrade.htm), 10.

p. 110, "irascible, forceful, an expert . . ." Halberstam, *The
Best and the Brightest*, 473.

p. 110, "as a man willing . . ." Ibid.

p. 110, "I think we are kidding the world . . ." *Naval History
Magazine*, (http://www.usni.org/navalhistory/Articles99/
NHandrade.htm), 10.

p. 110, "deliberate and unprovoked" Young, *The Vietnam
Wars 1945-1990*, 120.

p. 110, "routine patrol in international waters" Ibid.

p. 110, "Our navy played absolutely no part . . ." Ibid.

p. 110, "Hell, Wayne, you can't get in a fight . . ." Ibid.

p. 111, "the kind of president . . ." Ibid.

p. 111, "all necessary measures" George C. Herring, *The
Pentagon Papers* Abridged Edition, (New York: McGraw-
Hill, 1993), 85.

p. 111, "I believe that history will record . . ." Halberstam, *The
Best and the Brightest*, 475-76.

p. 113, "Many of the people who . . ." McNamara, *In Retrospect*, 140.

p. 114, "the incidents..." Ibid.

p. 114, "In simple terms . . ." Ibid., 140-41.

p. 115, "The idea that the Johnson administration . . ." Ibid.,
141.

p. 115, "The problem was not . . ." Ibid.

Afterword
p. 116, "more certain than ever . . ." Karnow, *Vietnam*, 561.
p. 118, "the only person in the world . . ." Schreadley, *From the Rivers to the Sea*, 72.
p. 118, "best and brightest" Ibid.
p. 118, "What the hell kind of scale . . ." Ibid.
p. 119, "Those Whiz Kids . . ." Ibid.
p. 119, "should a president take our nation to war . . ." McNamara, *In Retrospect*, 142-43.

Bibliography

Websites

Gulf of Tonkin Notebook.
   http://members.aol.com/warlibrary/vwton.htm

Naval History Magazine.
   http://www.usni.org/navalhistory/Articles99/
   NHandrade.htm

The Cold War: Episode 11: Vietnam.
   http://www.gwu.edu/~nsarchiv/coldwar/interviews/
   episode-11/stockdale1.html

Books

Asprey, Robert B. *War in the Shadows: The Guerrilla in History*. Vol. 2. Garden City, NY: Doubleday, 1975.

Beschloss, Michael. *Reaching for Glory: Lyndon Johnson's Secret White House Tapes, 1964-1965*. New York: Simon & Schuster, 2001.

Bird, Kai. *The Color of Truth: McGeorge Bundy and William Bundy: Brothers in Arms: A Biography*. New York: Simon & Schuster, 1998.

Bonds, Ray, ed. *The Vietnam War: The Illustrated History of the Conflict in Southeast Asia*. Rev. ed. New York: Crown Publishers, 1983.

Bosiljevic, T.L. *Seals: UDT/Seal Operations in Vietnam*. New York: Ivy Books, 1990.

Boyer, Paul S., ed. *The Oxford Companion to United States History*. New York: Oxford University Press, 2001.

Burkett, B.G. and Glenna Whitley. *Stolen Valor: How the Vietnam Generation Was Robbed of Its Heroes and Its History*. Dallas: Verity Press, 1998.

Chambers II, John Whiteclay, ed. *The Oxford Companion to American Military History*. New York: Oxford University Press, 1999.

Clodfelter, Mark. *The Limits of Airpower: The American Bombing of North Vietnam*. New York: Free Press, 1989.

Conboy, Kenneth, and Dale Andradé. *Spies and Commandos: How America Lost the Secret War in North Vietnam*. Lawrence, KS: University Press of Kansas, 2000.

Cowley, Robert, and Geoffrey Parker, eds. *The Reader's Companion to Military History*. Boston: Houghton Mifflin, 1996.

Cutler, Thomas J. *Brown Water, Black Berets: Coastal and Riverine Warfare in Vietnam*. Annapolis: Naval Institute Press, 1988.

Davidson, Phillip B. *Vietnam at War: The History: 1946-1975*. New York: Oxford University Press, 1991.

Doyle, Edward, Samuel Lipsman, and the editors of Boston Publishing Company. *America Takes Over*. The Vietnam Experience series. Editor-in-Chief Robert Manning. Boston: Boston Publishing, 1982.

Duiker, William J. *Ho Chi Minh*. New York: Hyperion, 2000.

Dunnigan, James F., and Albert A. Nofi. *Dirty Little Secrets of the Vietnam War*. New York: St. Martin's Press, 1999.

Fall, Bernard. *Hell in a Very Small Place: The Siege of Dien Bien Phu*. Philadelphia: J.B. Lippincott, 1967.

————. *Street Without Joy: The Bloody Road to Dien Bien Phu*. Mechanicsburg, PA: Stackpole Books, 1994.

Fitzgerald, Frances. *Fire in the Lake: The Vietnamese and the Americans in Vietnam*. Boston: Little, Brown, 1972.

Freedman, Lawrence. *Kennedy's Wars: Berlin, Cuba, Laos, and Vietnam*. New York: Oxford University Press, 2000.

Friedman, Norman. *The Fifty-Year War: Conflict and Strategy in the Cold War*. Annapolis: Naval Institute Press, 2000.

Gardner, Lloyd C. *Pay Any Price: Lyndon Johnson and the Wars for Vietnam*. Chicgao: Ivan R. Dee, 1995.

Goldstein, Donald M., Katherine V. Dillon, and J. Michael Wenger. *The Vietnam War: The Story and the Photographs*. Herndon, VA: Brassey's, 1999.

Halberstam, David. *The Best and the Brightest*. Modern Library Edition. New York: Random House, 2001.

Hammond, William M. *Reporting Vietnam: Media and Military at War*. Lawrence, KS: University Press of Kansas, 1998.

Herring, George C. *The Pentagon Papers*. Abridged Edition. New York: McGraw-Hill, 1993.

Holmes, Richard, ed. *The Oxford Companion to Military History*. New York: Oxford University Press, 2001.

Isaacs, Jeremy, and Taylor Downing. *Cold War: An Illustrated History, 1945-1991*. Boston: Little, Brown, 1998.

Kaiser, David. *American Tragedy: Kennedy, Johnson, and the Origins of the Vietnam War*. Cambridge, MA: Belknap Press of Harvard University Press, 2000.

Karnow, Stanley. *Vietnam: A History*. Rev. ed. New York: Viking, 1991.

Kimball, Jeffrey. *Nixon's Vietnam War*. Lawrence, KS: University Press of Kansas, 1998.

Kutler, Stanley I. *Encyclopedia of the Vietnam War*. New York: Simon & Schuster Macmillan, 1996.

Leckie, Robert. *The Wars of America*. New and Updated Ed. Vol. 2: From 1900 to 1992. New York: HarperCollins*Publishers*, 1992.

The Library of America. *Reporting Vietnam*. Part One: American Journalism 1959-1969. New York: Literary Classics of the United States, 1998.

————. *Reporting Vietnam*. Part Two: American Journalism 1969-1975. New York: Literary Classics of the United States, 1998.

Logevall, Fredrik. *Choosing War: The Lost Chance for Peace and the Escalation of War in Vietnam*. Berkeley, CA: University of California Press, 1999.

McNamara, Robert S., with Brian VanDeMark. *In Retrospect: The Tragedy and Lessons of Vietnam*. New York: Times Books, 1995.

McNamara, Robert S., James G. Blight, Robert K. Brigham, et al. *Argument Without End: In Search of Answers to the Vietnam Tragedy*. New York: Public Affairs, 1999.

Mann, Robert. *A Grand Delusion: America's Descent into Vietnam*. New York: Basic Books, 2001.

Margiotta, Franklin D., ed. *Brassey's Encyclopedia of Military History and Biography*. Washington, DC: Brassey's, 1994.

Matloff, Maurice, ed. *American Military History*. Vol. 2: 1902-1996. Conshohocken, PA: Combuned Books, 1996.

Michel III, Marshall L. *Clashes: Air Combat over North Vietnam 1965-1972*. Annapolis: Naval Institute Press, 1997.

Moïse, Edwin E. *Tonkin Gulf and the Escalation of the Vietnam War*. Chapel Hill, NC: University of North Carolina Press, 1996.

Nalty, Bernard, ed. *The Vietnam War: The History of America's Conflict in Southeast Asia*. Classic Conflicts series. London: Salamander Books, 1998.

Page, Tim and John Pimlott, eds. *NAM: The Vietnam Experience 1965-75*. New York: Mallard Press, 1990.

Parrish, Thomas. *The Cold War Encyclopedia.* New York: Henry Holt, 1996.

Pimlott, John. *Vietnam: The Decisive Battles.* New York: Macmillan, 1990.

Plaster, John L. *SOG: The Secret Wars of America's Commandos in Vietnam.* New York: Penguin Putnam, 1998.

Powaski, Ronald E. *The Cold War: The United States and the Soviet Union, 1917-1991.* New York: Oxford University Press, 1998.

Prados, John. *The Hidden History of the Vietnam War.* Chicago: Ivan R. Dee, 1998.

Rice Jr., Earle. *The Tet Offensive.* San Diego: Lucent Books, 1997.

Schreadley, R.L. *From the Rivers to the Sea: The U.S. Navy in Vietnam.* Annapolis: Naval Institute Press, 1992.

Schultz, Jr., Richard H. *The Secret War Against Hanoi: Kennedy's and Johnson's Use of Spies, Saboteurs, and Covert Warriors in North Vietnam.* New York: HarperCollins*Publishers*, 1999.

Schwarzkopf, H. Norman with Peter Petre. *It Doesn't Take a Hero: General H. Norman Schwarzkopf: The Autobiography.* New York: Bantam Books, 1992.

Sheehan, Neil. *A Bright Shining Lie: John Paul Vann and America in Vietnam.* New York: Random House, 1989.

Siff, Ezra Y. *Why the Senate Slept: The Gulf of Tonkin Resolution and the Beginning of America's Vietnam War.* Westport, CT: Praeger, 1999.

Smith, John T. *The Linebacker Raids: The Bombing of North Vietnam, 1972.* London: Arms and Armour Press, 1998.

Spector, Ronald H. *At War at Sea: Sailors and Naval Combat in the Twentieth Century.* New York: Viking, 2001.

Summers Jr., Harry G. *Vietnam War Almanac.* New York: Facts On File, 1985.

————. *On Strategy: A Critical Analysis of the Vietnam War*. Novato, CA: Presidio Press, 1995.

————. *Historical Atlas of the Vietnam War*. Boston: Houghton Mifflin, 1995.

Trest, Warren A. *Air Commando One: Heinie Aderholt and America's Secret Air Wars*. Washington: Smithsonian Institution Press, 2000.

Tucker, Spencer C., ed. *Encyclopedia of the Vietnam War: A Political, Social, and Military History*. New York: Oxford University Press, 1998.

Young, Marilyn. *The Vietnam Wars 1945-1990*. New York: HarperCollins*Publishers*, 1991.

Websites

Anti-Communist Credentialism. Blaine Taylor. The History Net.
http://www.thehistorynet.com/Vietnam/articles/1999/08992_text.htm.

By Sea, Air, and Land. An illustrated history of the U.S. Navy and the war in Southeast Asia.
http://www.history.navy.mil/seairland/chap2.htm.

New Light on the Gulf of Tonkin. Captain Ronnie E. Ford, U.S. Army. The History Net.
http://www.thehistorynet.com/Vietnam/articles/1997/08972_text.htm.

PTF Nasty–History. http://www.ptfnasty.com/ptfHistory.html.

The Relevance of the Tonkin Gulf Incidents: U.S. Military Action in Vietnam, August 1964. Kim Weitzman.
http://www.ttu.edu/~vietnam/96papers/maddox4.htm.

The Tonkin Gulf Incident; 1964. The Avalon Project at the Yale Law School.
http://www.yale.edu/lawweb/avalon/tonkin-g.htm.

Index